Praise for A Ga

Entertaining, funny and
characters from history. Recommended. – David Gee, novelist

Congratulations on such a great book! I really liked the comical ones,
especially the one with Ernest Shackleton's brother in it. The por-
trayal of Radclyffe Hall is a hoot! – Mickey Silver, novelist

Praise for Amiable Warriors, Volume 1

He demonstrates an absolute flare for bringing to exhilarating life a
subject that, in the wrong hands, could have been an encyclopaedia
of events and participants. The book is bursting with fascinating testi-
monies, oral and written, from people who were a part of CHE. It is
of huge importance that the author has captured so much personal
testimony as, with time passing as it does, these accounts might other-
wise be lost forever. Despite 'not being an historian' Scott-Presland
gives a meticulously detailed account of the way in which, despite
immense obstacles, the criminalised [in the case of gay men] and mar-
ginalised built a movement that gradually helped to provide LGBT
people with a voice and a platform – Hannah Snow, Amazon

Amazing read, well-documented and written, would recommend.
– Kazzi, Amazon

An almost Dickensian flavour... a work of considerable social
importance. – Prof. Jeffrey Weekes, Emeritus Professor, South
Bank University

A Gay Century

A Gay Century: Volume Two: 1973–2001

Published by The Conrad Press Ltd. in the United Kingdom 2022

Tel: +44(0)1227 472 874
www.theconradpress.com
info@theconradpress.com

ISBN 978-1-915494-30-6

Printed and bound in Great Britain by Clays Ltd, Elcograf S.p.A

Typesetting and cover design by The Book Typesetters
www.thebooktypesetters.com

This book has been typeset in Adobe Garamond Pro, Gill Sans MT and Berlin Sans FB

Illustrations by David Shenton

The Conrad Press logo was designed by Maria Priestley.

A Gay Century

Volume Two: 1973–2001

Peter Scott-Presland

Contents

To Gökhan, without whom...

Introduction

For those who haven't read Volume One, *A Gay Century* is a series of 17 snapshots of what Gay life was like across the decades of the twentieth century. I say 'Gay', because this is mainly about gay men, although in Volume One we had the notable lesbians Radclyffe Hall, of *Well of Loneliness* fame, and Esmé Langley, founder of *Arena 3* and other pioneering lesbian organisations. In Volume Two we have the lesbian couple Lou and Bev in *A Shot at the Future*. Despite this, the boys steal the scene – as usual.

These scenarios were written to be set to music by Robert Ely, a cycle of mainly one-act operas which could be performed by small-scale companies, often 'pop-up' companies, using a minimum of resources. Shorn of their music, they were performed on Zoom over 2020–2021 and have since been posted on YouTube.

What to call them? 'Libretti' sounds intimidating, or possibly like Italian sweets. 'Texts' reeks of art-house pretension and Arts Council grants. They're mostly too short to be called plays proper. They are more than sketches, though. I settled on 'vignettes', as having a lavender-scented charm. In this I was influenced by Laurence Housman's series of short plays about Queen Victoria spread over several volumes, including *Palace Plays* and *Happy and Glorious*. The concept of a gay century I nicked from *Untold Decades* by the great and unjustly neglected [at least in England] gay playwright, the American Robert Patrick.

The second volume of plays which make up *A Gay Century* kicks off in 1973. This means that all the plays here take place within my lifetime as an adult gay man; although I appreciate that to a younger gender-fluid audience even the A.I.D.S. pandemic of the 80s and 90s now seems as remote and 'historical' as the Oscar Wilde trial.

In this second period we turn away from well-known historical figures to the 'gay in the street'. This is because the lives of 'ordinary' gays [is there such a thing as an ordinary gay life?] come increasingly into focus, where previously much of our knowledge came from the biographies of the rich and famous – or from court records. In so turning we come up against the issues which have been of major concern to campaigners for civil rights – the treatment of vulnerable older people in *November*, gays in the military in *After Sefton*, the A.I.D.S. pandemic and its threats to civil liberties in *Quarantine*, parenting for lesbians and gays in *A Shot at the Future*, Section 28 in *Eric Lives with Martin and Jenny*, and, in *Skin Deep*, violence. It culminates in a quieter retrospective of the century from the perspective of two of our 'ordinary gays', whose main contribution to any struggle has been to get on quietly with their own lives without much concealment, and so lead by example.

It is notable that the plays in this volume tend to be longer than the ones in the first; only seven, compared to ten. I suspect this is because, since I am writing about my own times, it is more difficult for me to distil in the same way. Unlike the first volume, this contains no references, because little research was required: it was all there in anecdote and lived experience.

In coming closer to the present, the language of the cycle has changed. Because less distant in time, it has become more demotic, more recognisably 'ours', and this in itself has presented more of a challenge to make it 'singable', and for Robert Ely the composer to set to music. The self-consciously 'poetic' would in this context sound false, so I have tried to heighten certain moments as Arias, Duets and Quartets in traditional style, and to heighten language within those moments, including the sparing use of rhyme, but without going over the top. Between times the 'recitative' is casual, almost slangy. We have before us recent examples of colloquial play-to-opera in *A Streetcar Named Desire*, *The Silver Tassie* and *Miss Julie*, to name but three.

Nor is it unknown to publish opera librettos in play form. The protean French polymath Boris Vian published a book of Operas, including *Fiesta* which was set by Darius Milhaud, and several unperformed libretti; while the librettos of Benjamin Britten operas are collected in a single volume – and this is not so you can understand the stories when you are listening to the music; they can be read and appreciated as drama in their own right. It goes to support my contention that there are no great operas without great librettos.

The other element which presents more challenges is the role of popular music in the cycle. It is inconceivable that one could write a cycle like this without reference to the popular music of the time, which homosexuals of every era would have drunk to, danced to, and cruised to. In the earlier part of the century, this would have included the works of popular composers such as Kurt Weill and Ivor Novello, who have now become 'classical'.

Here, in *1973: November*, we have a bridge between two eras, in a central character who is an octogenarian performer whose heyday was in the 1920s.

It is in *Quarantine* and *Skin Deep* that we enter the world of electric pop and dance music, and a style a world away from a trio or quartet of conventional acoustic instruments. Robert has yet to set most of the later pieces, so this is a bridge we shall cross when we get to it – hopefully not a bridge too far.

As before, we have aimed our work at the numerous brave pop-up opera companies which operate on a shoestring all over the country, presenting music theatre in the most unlikely venues: restaurants, shopping malls, factories, lavatories, parks. These are slim-line operas, requiring no more than seven performers in all; though it must be admitted that as a result of our self-imposed strait-jacket, *Quarantine* in particular demands the most startling versatility and quick-change ability from its singers.

I must repeat, these are primarily opera librettos which happen to work as short plays and are intended to be sung. In writing them, I have found this constraint has brought a strict discipline to my writing which may have been lacking earlier. When you know something is to be sung, you turn every phrase over in your mouth, you taste it almost as a physical object. Do the lips and the tongue have to do too much travelling? Is there a rhythm to it? Is a long vowel being cramped? Can we get rid of words? It makes for a directness and economy which greatly helps the drama. Robert Ely has also given invaluable assistance when pointing out what works with music, and what doesn't.

I have been asked many times why I haven't included certain subjects, such as education, or housing, or losing your job. An opera is not a 'subject' but a story with characters. For the purpose of this project, it is a story which has maybe three characters, and can be told in the space of an hour. And, more nebulously, that story must lend itself to musical treatment. There are many well-known gay historical figures and scenes that have equally been left out because they are too long, too baggy, have too many characters to tell the story, or feel inherently 'unmusical'.

The one issue which has emerged in the 21st century which has created a gulf with the past which many young people find difficult to bridge is that of gender, rather than sexuality, and of identity politics. The most obvious example of this is the still-to-be-resolved issue of transgender rights. This seems to be much more contentious concerning transition from male to female than from female to male; I suspect this is something to do with the inherent power and attraction perceived in traditional male roles. I won't elaborate on that because I'm sure to offend someone; we are all walking on eggshells in this field.

A contemporary young person is more likely to be out of sympathy with any struggle over the right to express one's sexuality with a person of the same biological gender – increasing numbers of young people are saying that they don't define their own gender in binary terms, they don't look for a partner on the same basis, and in any case, they don't regard having sex as particularly important – indeed they would rather not have it. They acknowledge that the struggle happened, they just don't see that it has much to do with them.

Nevertheless, it happened, and it was what gave our lives definition and meaning through the twentieth century. I stress again, these are works of fiction and imagination, not historical fact. However, historical truth and historical fact are not necessarily the same thing, and the playlets in *A Gay Century: Volume Two* remain true to the spirit of their times.

Peter Scott-Presland
December 2022

A Gay Century: 11

1973: Autumn

A two-act chamber opera

A story of November and May

Above: *1972 Gay Liberation Front Rally at Trafalgar Square*
Below: *Quentin Crisp*

Introduction

1 969–73 were the years of a tipping point in the way gay people regarded themselves. In the wake of the Stonewall Riots[1] in New York, when customers of a seedy mafia-run bar for gay men, lesbians and transsexuals finally called time on endless police raids, shakedowns and other harassment, Americans formed the Gay Liberation Front [G.L.F.] to say 'Enough is Enough'. It was inspired by the hippy counter-culture and the black power movement, as an essential tool for self-realisation, and for formulating political action.

It was brought to London by two young students, Bob Mellor and Aubrey Walter, in the summer/autumn of 1970, and quickly spread, especially on student campuses. Although there had been earlier moves to advocate gay rights, this was a sea-change: it was revolutionary, it offered a critique of the whole nature of society and the economic system it supported, and it saw itself in an alliance with both women's and black liberation. It also spawned a variety of cultural and self-help projects. It only lasted about three years, though its ideas still reverberate. But brief though it was, bliss was it in that dawn to be alive.

There were certain *monstres sacrés* to the G.L.F., and fore-

---

[1] It is more customary these days to refer to the Stonewall Rebellion or Stonewall Uprising. In my opinion this implies something altogether more considered than what actually happened. 'Riot' conveys the raw fury, the urge to destroy the oppressor and all his works, and – yes! – the excitement of it.

most amongst them was Quentin Crisp. Dazzling in his self-confidence and sense of style, he yet epitomised many of the worst aspects of what we were beginning to think of as self-oppression: his insistence that homosexuals could never be fulfilled because we were destined only to fall in love with 'real', i.e. straight, men ['there is no tall dark man']; his to us pathetic assertions that there was nothing to be proud of in being homosexual, and his complete indifference bordering on antipathy towards Gay Rights. This was seen as hypocrisy, in that he derived quite a lot of his income from appearing in gay venues and acting as Grand Marshall on various Gay Pride Marches. He made things worse for himself in the 1990s when he described A.I.D.S. as a fad and homosexuality itself as a disease.

And yet... and yet... his very existence was a manifestation of gay pride, and the assertion of his unique essence in the face of ongoing and vicious queer-bashing displayed a courage most of us could only aspire to. The henna, the nail varnish, the make-up, the scarves were all the politest of two fingers to conventional values. He would be anything you wanted him to be, say what you expected him to say, to the point where he had little personality as such. For all his openness to people, you could never get to know him. It was all passive-aggressive; his composure and self-containment were terrifying.

He was a product of the 1920s. Another offspring of that bygone age was the now almost forgotten figure of Douglas Byng. Byng was the foremost cabaret star of the 1920s–1950s. In one picture of Piccadilly Circus/Coventry Street his name is seen up in huge lights over the Café de Paris – with Marlene Dietrich in tiny letters at the bottom as next week's act. Byng was born in 1893, the same year as Ivor Novello, but lived on well into his 90s.

Byng's cabaret act was female impersonation, his brightest creations were pantomime dames. However, in revue and cabaret, his drag was often suggested by the merest hint of costume or prop. I was a friend of his agent, a lovely, gentle man called Patrick Newley. Patrick persuaded Dougie to appear at a gay pub called *The Cricketers* in Battersea in 1984. It was meant to be only a Personal Appearance, but he couldn't resist doing three or four numbers. A tea towel on the head and he was Queen Victoria; a bit of tartan for Flora MacDonald. He was in a velvet suit, but the audience could watch him transform himself in less than a minute. The fascinating thing was that offstage he had the most violent facial tic. Onstage the spasm disappeared completely.

During the Second World War, Byng billed himself as 'bawdy but British', but bawdy was too broad a term for what he did. He could use the dirtiest gay slang, but never cause the slightest offence. He got away with it for three reasons: a] it was in the mouths of female characters; b] it was completely po-faced; c] he had a priceless gift for placing words for maximum comic impact. Some lines still make me smile even as I think of them:

'Flora MacDonald, Flora MacDonald,
Heavy wi' haggis and dripping with dew…'

'I'm Doris, the Goddess of Wind…
I blow through the bedrooms and blow out the light,

I blow to the left and I blow to the right;
My life's just one blow through from morning to night –
It's the wind, it's the wind!'

You can find several examples of his work on YouTube; perhaps the most outrageous is with Lance Lister as The Cabaret Boys.

https://www.youtube.com/watch?v=IE58CHZfJLo

In 1970 the Gay Liberation Front held its first meetings in London[2], and the ideas imported from the United States of coming out as personal liberation started to take root. The next two years were heady indeed, an explosion of energy and activism; however as in many revolutions without hierarchy, the fireworks went off in all directions, and factions soon emerged. The radical feminists [Rad. Fems.] insisted that only by relinquishing all the trappings of masculinity could true liberation be found; others saw the way forward as being in alliance with the militant left and with black power. Some people were concerned with making the lives of gay men better in the short term – helplines, advice, a defence fund for men arrested for sex offences, reducing the age of consent to sixteen. To others this was only a sticking plaster, and it was actually better to allow injustices to proliferate, and to fan the flames of discontent until they erupted in full-scale anger and riots. All agreed, however, that the nuclear family was the root cause of gay oppression, and it was far better to live and share communally. For a good if partial account of the period,

---

[2] At the London School of Economics.

read Stuart Feather's *Blowing the Lid*.

https://www.amazon.co.uk/Blowing-Lid-Liberation-Revolution-Radical/dp/1785351435

By 1973 the various G.L.F. fragments were not speaking much to each other. But communes were alive and well, especially Bethnal Rouge in East London. Douglas Byng was 80, and almost totally forgotten. Put the two facts together, move the composite Crisp/Byng figure into a council flat in Poplar, and – *voila!* – the makings of a particular kind of culture clash. Factor in also a concern which is contemporary in 2019 but then would not have been high on anyone's list of priorities: the situation of older LGBT people, largely on their own, battling isolation and increasing infirmity, facing the prospect of heterosexist and hetero-normative old people's homes, and having to go back into the closet because of their dependency on carers who might be as prejudiced as the rest of society.

What kind of responsibility do LGBT+ young people have to their elders, individually or collectively? Is it enough to collect their tales of earlier times to garland history, or does caring and respect involve something more than that? Something more than putting money into the collection box? Put it this way: would you want an old queer living with you, teetering on the edge of incontinence and dementia? Especially if they held the reactionary views of someone like Crisp?

Because of the sea changes in our lives in these years, and the significance of the issues to our culture, *Autumn* is longer than average, and is one of the pieces which merits an interval. It plays at about 85 minutes.

The characters are all fictional, but take elements from life. Valentine de Vere is a composite of Crisp and Byng; Penny Dreadful draws on Lavinia Co-op, a member of the old Bloolips Theatre, whom I saw recently at the Royal Vauxhall Tavern in a play about old gay men. Vinnie is solid down-to-earth working-class, and very savvy; I imagine him when young being rather more naïve. Walter Craig, here of the Marxist wing of G.L.F., was based on Warren Haig, one of the most dynamic and articulate of the 'straight-gay' faction. Warren was an absolute gift as a media spokesperson, a great theoretician, but somewhat aloof from the day-to-day business of running an office, building a movement, organising a dance or a demo, etc. etc. He was an American, worked in Compendium Books in Camden, and had one of the most comprehensive address books in London. His disappearance from London in the later 1970s was sudden and unexplained. Many people would love to know whether he is still alive. And how he is.

Mrs. Goodhart? I think we all know a Mrs Goodhart. Bless her.

When I sent the libretto to Robert, my composer on the project, he emailed me back to ask where he could find the Valentine de Vere [Douglas Byng] songs, because they were not on YouTube. I had to tell him, that these are not Byng songs, but pastiches – *homages*, rather – and I hope I've done the naughty old boy justice.

CAST

VALENTINE DE VERE: Baritone

Male, 81, a former cabaret star, a queen with a strong sense of style. Always impeccable, though the effect is now achieved at great cost. Always behaves as if he is onstage. He is playing the part of Valentine de Vere.

PENNY DREADFUL: Counter-Tenor

Male, 21, a member of the Gay Liberation Front [G.L.F.], a Rad. Fem. [radical feminist], whose life and dress is a guerilla war against masculinity. He is new to the movement, enthusiastic, but a bit naïve. Cockney. Torn between hero-worship of Warren and an urge to send him up.

WALTER CRAIG: Baritone

Male, 27, American, a member of G.L.F., but of the Marxist wing. His life is largely taken up with meetings, and with demonstrations in solidarity with other oppressed groups. A tendency to harangue. Little humour. Lover, in a rather offhand way, of Penny.

MRS GOODHART: Mezzo-Soprano

Early 40s, a Council social worker. She exudes motherly concern, of a rather bossy kind. Her heavy caseload means that her mind is often elsewhere, and she seeks the easiest solution, the line of least resistance, to difficulties.

SETTING

Autumn 1973

De Vere's run-down council flat in Poplar; a clothing rack with stage costumes for his famous song characters – Clarissa of the Quays, Bertha of the Blackout, Bossy Flossy Nightingale, Vicky the Grumpy Old Queen. An old chintz armchair, a table with a wind-up gramophone. Other chairs as needed. A full-length mirror. There is a door, the other side of which is the outside balcony.

INSTRUMENTS

Piano trio: piano, violin, cello; piano solo for de Vere's songs.

AUTUMN

Scene One

[There is a record playing on the gramophone. De VERE is lying face down on the floor, half-dressed. Before passing out, he was in the process of bandaging his poor ulcerated legs. One is done, the bandage falls away from the other. A jar of E45 dermatological cream lies open by him. He is motionless.]

RECORD: They call me the idol of the dockyards,
            Cos there's no-one more idle, dear, than
                me.
            When there's lots of ropes to tie down
            I just have to have a lie-down –
            Work plays havoc with the coccyx, you'll
                agree.
            When dockers all rush to and fro,
            I tell those dockers where to go –
            [Very deep:] Try to get them down below:
            I'm Clarissa of the Quays!
            Clarissa of the Quays!
            When ships heave to, let joy be uncon-
                trolled.
            In ones and twos and threes,
            From o'er the seven seas,
            Can't wait to let them get me in their
                hold.
            Clarissa of the Quays!
            Clarissa of the Quays!

Welcome to the dockyard,
Where you'll find me on me knees.
I'm such an eager scrubber,
And I'm trying hard to please.
You could say that scrubbing's my voca-
    tion and my passion;
I'm the only bit of meat that isn't on the
    ration[3].
Clarissa of the Quays!
Clarissa of the –
Clarissa of the –

[The record is stuck in the groove. After a few minutes there is a banging on the door.]

PENNY: *(offstage)* Mr de Vere! *[Pause.]*
                Mr de Vere! *[Pause.]*
                I know you're in there, I can hear the music.
                It's stuck in the groove.

WALTER: *(offstage)* Just like him, dreadful old man!

PENNY: *(offstage)* Don't be rude. He might be ill.
                Or hurt.

[More banging on the door.]

WALTER: *(offstage)* Mr de Vere, we're coming in.

---

[3] This line is a nod to Byng's *Blackout Bella*.

PENNY: Shouldn't we call the police?

WALTER: The fuzz? You must be joking!
              I got an ounce of pot on me.
              Anyway, we *never* call the police to *anything*.
              Now stand well back.

PENNY: You're so butch.

[The sound of a shoulder to the door. After a few blows, it gives way and WALTER falls into the room, followed by PENNY. PENNY goes to the gramophone and takes the needle off the record. WALTER looks around.]

WALTER: Jeez, what a dump!

PENNY: Look at these frocks! I told you he was a queen.

WALTER: Can't have been cleaned in years.
              [He looks off] I daren't go into the kitchen.

PENNY: This is real silk, you know.
              And the stitching is by hand.

[De VERE groans.]

WALTER: What are you doing looking at that stuff?
              There's a sick man here.

[He goes to de VERE, and tries to turn him over.]

PENNY: Shouldn't we call an ambulance?

De VERE: *[Faint]* No, no ambulance. I'll be fine.

WALTER: Here, let me help you.

[He lifts him towards the armchair.]

WALTER: Hey, you're heavy for an old broad.

De VERE: *[Instantly alert, touchy:]* That's quite
                    enough of that.
              My name is Valentine de Vere.
              Mister Valentine de Vere.
              There's nothing effeminate about me.

PENNY: That's telling him, girl. *[De VERE glares.]*
              Sorry, Mr. de Vere.

[WALTER goes into the kitchen.]

De VERE: And you are?

PENNY: Penny Dreadful.
              Not my real name, of course.
              My camp name, for the commune.
              We live in Pink Poplar –
              It's the squat on the corner,

What used to be the Post Office.

De VERE: We? You and…?

PENNY: His name is Walter. Walter Craig.

[WALTER returns with a glass of water. De VERE waves it aside.]

De VERE: There's a forty-year-old single malt
             In the medicine cabinet in the bathroom.
             If you would be so kind, Mr. Craig –
             I take it with water, fifty-fifty.

WALTER: But –

De VERE: I'm sure it will be much more thera-
                  peutic.
             [Stern behind smile.] If you please.
             [A battle of wills follows.]
             Thank you so much, Mr Craig.
             And do please get one for yourself –
             And for your – friend.

[WALTER exits again.]

De VERE: Mr Craig – he is your 'special friend', is
             he not?

PENNY: *[Shocked]* Of course not.

We don't believe in monogamy.

De VERE: What are you doing here?

PENNY: We're organising a children's party
              Down at the squat on Sunday, in the
                  garden.
              We've got a magician and everything.
              We were going round the estate
              To tell people about it,
              So they can send their children.

De VERE: Do you think they will?

PENNY: So far no-one's slammed the door on us.

*[De VERE has recovered enough to carry on applying his
bandages. He talks the while.]*

De VERE: You must forgive me,
              But since you came uninvited,
              You have to take me as you find me.
              I am never seen *au naturel* in public.
              My public for today
              Is Mrs Sandra Goodhart.
              Goodhart by name, Goodhart by nature –
              A well-meaning soul who means to tidy me
              Away into an old folk's home,
              Where she can forget about me.
              She'll tick me off her list, and let the flat

To a nice young Asian family.
But I will fight her all the way.

PENNY: What will you do?

De VERE: I will refuse to go.
                I will barricade myself in.

[WALTER re-enters with three glasses of scotch. They are generous doubles.]

WALTER: Did I hear the word barricade?
                Do we have a revolutionary here?

PENNY: The council wants to chuck him out.

De VERE: They will not succeed.

[WALTER gives him his scotch, and PENNY hers.]

De VERE: Thank you, Mr Craig.

[PENNY knocks hers back. Coughs.]

De VERE: Mr. Dreadful, you have just
                Poured ten shillings down your throat.

PENNY: Blimey, that's four pints of beer.

De VERE: I was given that bottle

In nineteen-fifty-two
By Maurice Chevalier,
After the Royal Variety Performance.

PENNY: Get away!

[Over the dialogue, De VERE has finished bandaging his legs, and pulls up a pair of deep purple velvet trousers. He smooths his shirt down.]

De VERE: He did not mean me to give it away
For someone to knock back
Like orange squash.
Look at Mr Craig,
Follow his example.
He knows how to sip it,
To roll it round his mouth –

PENNY: You've rolled it round your mouth
A few times, aintcha girl?

De VERE: I could tell he was a member
Of the aristocracy.

WALTER: I am not, not at all.

De VERE: The aristocracy of America,
The aristocracy of money.
Over your Che Guevara T-shirt
You sport a bespoke Harris Tweed

Herringbone jacket
Which cost a good
Hundred and thirty pounds.
I'm sure those working boots
You bought in Jermyn Street.
Am I right?
[To PENNY:] Pass me those socks…

[PENNY does so.]

PENNY: Are those real silk?

De VERE: They are.

[PENNY puts a finger through a hole in it.]

Ignore the hole.
A gentleman never draws attention to his
  hole.

[De VERE has made a very naughty double entendre and knows it, but remains po-faced. PENNY splutters with laughter, but De VERE's manner forces him to keep a straight face, which makes it funnier. It is a moment of bonding. De VERE indicates WALTER's boots.]

De VERE: Jermyn Street? Am I right?

WALTER: Well…

De VERE: And made to measure?

WALTER: If you must know…
             My parents lived in Boston,
             In Beacon Hill;
             The Hamptons in summer.
             They were what was called Old Money,
             Planters of untold wealth,
             Of vast lands and slaves —
             And I hate it! Hate it!

[De VERE is pulling on some well-worn, but well-polished elastic-sided shoes.]

PENNY: Why d'you think he goes with me?
             Common as muck, me.
             He's hoping it will rub off.

WALTER: I spend it as fast as I can,
             But it feels like I can never catch up.

PENNY: Thanks to Walter,
             We're the best appointed squat
             East of Bethnal Green.
             Hot and cold, with central heating,
             He's ever so generous,
             We always go to demos
             In his Lamborghini.

WALTER: You can borrow it if you like.

[De VERE has finished getting his shoes on. He indicates the purple velvet suit jacket. PENNY brings it, and puts it on him, smoothing down the shoulders. For a moment de VERE is back in the theatre and PENNY is his dresser.]

De VERE: I have never learnt to drive.
            I always had a chauffeur
            When I needed one.

[He looks in the mirror. He takes a silk scarf and throws it over his shoulder. Arranges it.]

WALTER: Well, maybe we can drive you.

PENNY: The only place Walter drives you is insane.

WALTER: Maybe we can take you to a Gay Day.

De VERE: A what?

WALTER: A Gay Day. It's like a picnic,
            But with Pride.

PENNY: We got these letters
            Sewn on sacks with sequins.
            Everybody wears a different-coloured
               letter —

WALTER: They spell out GAY LIBERATION.

PENNY: I'm always the 'G' –
           I like to be on the end –
           And the colour matches my skin tones.

[De VERE has taken a large Victorian diamond brooch and pinned it to his scarf. He wheels and faces them.]

De VERE: Mr. Craig, Mr Dreadful –
           You have been most kind,
           But now I must ask you to leave.

WALTER: We want to support you
           In your fight with the fascists on the
               council.

PENNY: Sisterhood is powerful.

De VERE: Exactly what do you think I am?

PENNY: *[Indicating de VERE's outfit.]* It's obvious,
               innit?

De VERE: What is obvious, Mr Dreadful?

PENNY: Well look at yourself…
           You must be gay!

De VERE: There it goes again!
           Why did they ruin that pretty little word?
           When I was young we had gay parties,

And they were gay affairs.
It was a light, transparent word,
Gossamer and sparkling.
What do we have now?
Gay Rights. Gay Power.
Heavy. Worthy.
Self-righteous. Dull.

[A bell rings before they can reply.]

De VERE: Ah, my public awaits.
Bring on the chorus girls,
Let the show commence!

[He has transformed, become larger than life. He exits.]

WALTER: What a hideous monument
To the bad old days –
A prime example of self-oppression.

PENNY: I think he's rather sweet.
I think he'd like our Fairy Frolics.

[De VERE re-enters with MRS GOODHART.]

De VERE: You must excuse the state
Of the State Apartments,
Mrs Goodhart.
The chambermaid has not had time to tidy.
Be seated, please.

La mia casa è la tua casa.

WALTER: That's Italian – my house is your house.

PENNY: I know. I've had enough Italian waiters.

MRS GOODHART: I won't beat about the bush,
Mr de Vere –

De VERE: Please, Mrs Goodhart,
Don't stand on formality.
Call me Valentine.

MRS. G: *[Playful in an elephantine way:]*
Now, Mr de Vere, don't try to distract me
With your charm. You know why I'm here –

De VERE: Charm? Would I be so underhand?
[To the others:] Have you ever known me
to be 'charming'?

[They shake their heads in unison.]

MRS. G: Who are they? Are they your next of kin?

De VERE: I have no next of kin,
My sister died three years ago.
She did not approve of me.

WALTER: We're only neighbours who were concerned –

PENNY: We could be next of kin –

WALTER: Shut up –

MRS. G: Concerned? What about?
            [To de VERE:] Have you had one of your
                turns again?
            [To the others:] He passed out a week ago,
            Left the gas on under a pot of soup.
            The smoke was pouring out of the flat.
            Next door called the caretaker,
            The caretaker called the fire brigade,
            The fire brigade called an ambulance.

De VERE: All that fuss. There was no harm.
            I didn't even have to throw away the
                saucepan.

MRS. G: You were unconscious for at least an hour.
            All that fuss and worry you caused!

De VERE: I was asleep. I had had a bad night.

PENNY: I have those –
            Especially after a night on the juice –

WALTER: With one of those Italian waiters –

[PENNY glares.]

MRS. G: You can make all the excuses you like,
           Mr de Vere. That won't change the fact –
           You're a danger to yourself,
           You're a danger to others.
           You're a fire hazard!

De VERE: I don't think so.
           Velvet is quite fire retardant –
           I can spray it with borax,
           If you insist.

MRS. G: This is no laughing matter.
           Don't you see, Mr de Vere,
           I'm worried about you.
           Look at the state of your flat –
           The dirt is inches deep!

De VERE: And has been for years. So what?
           The rubbish goes out regularly.
           There are no crumbs or scraps
           For cockroaches or mice.

MRS. G: Only because you hardly feed yourself.
           Look at you, you're skin and bone.
           You only live on soup and crackers.
           I've seen the empty tins in your bin.

De VERE: I eat within my means,
           So I can drink above them.
           Champagne, anyone?

WALTER: What right do you have
             To order this man around?

MRS. G: Who are these men?
             Are they friends of yours?

De VERE: *[Confused]* I don't quite rightly know.
             They came in and rescued me from the
                 floor.
             This is Mr Craig, this is Mr Dreadful.
             Mr Craig is some kind of revolutionary,
             I believe. Mr Dreadful is – Mr Dreadful.

PENNY: We live in the squat. Pink Poplar.

MRS. G: The one the neighbours all complain about.
             The Council has been trying to get you out.

PENNY: That rhymes! You're a poet!
             The neighbours don't all complain –
             We're putting on a children's party
             And nobody's objected.

MRS. G: But nobody will come. You'll see.

WALTER: Answer my question.
             By what right do you order him around?
             What arrogance asserts that you know
                 better
             Than he does what is good for him?

Benign despotism is not enough.

MRS. G: But we do know better.
            We have his interests at heart.
            When you get to Mr de Vere's age,
            You get confused. You cling
            To what you know, and what is comfortable –
            Even if it's killing you.

De VERE: Funny how I've now become invisible.
            Please don't talk about me
            As if I've left the room.

MRS. G: It *is* killing you. Can't you see that?

De VERE: And what's so very dreadful about death?
            People cling on so: to beauty, money, life.
            Life at all costs, 'We must have life.'
            Take the pills, run around, watch the
                weight;
            Cut out the booze, cut out the fat.
            Cut out the fun.

MRS. G: Do you really want to die, Mr de Vere?

De VERE: I would rather die than live a half-life.

MRS. G: Aren't you afraid to die?

De VERE: Why should I be?

MRS. G: I see, you believe in Heaven.

De VERE: Certainly not. I could not join a heavenly
                   choir,
               I am a natural soloist.

MRS. G: What do you think will happen to you
               If you stay here?

De VERE: I hope that I'll be sitting here like this –
               Probably on my own,
               But let us assume, for argument's sake,
               Talking to you. My heart will stop,
               My eyes glaze over,
               Perhaps I'll clutch my throat for breath.

[He does an elaborate comic re-enactment; we see for the first time his natural comic talent.]

               Then I will topple to the floor
               And I'll be gone,
               As if I'd never been here.
               Blackout, curtain, the end.
               You can drag the carcass out,
               Do with it what you will.
               In the words of my good friend, Leslie
                   Sarony,
               'Ain't it grand to be blooming well dead?'

MRS. G: *[Upset]* Don't you mind?

43

De VERE: Why should I mind? What is the point?
              Nobody can change it.
              Anger is so bad for the complexion.

MRS. G: What about your work? Your reputation?

De VERE: My reputation, such as it is,
              Will soon be buried in the sands of time.
              My work as distant as Dan Leno's.

WALTER: Who's Dan Leno?

PENNY: Hang on a jiff. What work?
              What reputation?

MRS. G: Don't you know?
              Valentine de Vere was a huge star
              Before the war. As big as Noël Coward.
              My mother thought him wonderful.

De VERE: And now to this we come. Eviction.

MRS. G: Removal to a place of safety.
              We have a lovely nursing home.
              You'll have the best of care,
              We'll feed you properly,
              Give you exercise,
              A singsong every week.

De VERE: What kind of songs?

I have no desire to know
The distance to Tipperary.

MRS. G: There is no point in carrying on like this,
            The authority has decided.
            You cannot go on living here,
            And that's an end to it.
            Your doctor agrees.

De VERE: What do doctors know?
            Mine thought I had cancer of the colon,
            When it was just a bad case of piles.
            He had a fatal stroke two days later.

WALTER: Surely we can fight this?

PENNY: There are lawyers come to G.L.F..

WALTER: We can find someone to speak on your
                behalf.

De VERE: That's one thing I have never needed.
            I have never been at a loss for words.

PENNY: Now, now. Don't be stubborn.

MRS. G: *[Getting up]* The decision has been made.
            I'm going now to get your doctor
            To sign the relevant forms.
            I'd advise you, Mr de Vere,

Get ready for the short journey –

De VERE: *[Hollow, dramatic:]* To the grave…

MRS. G: To the Cedars. It's very nice.
             You'll have a nice big room.
             You'll only share it with one other.

De VERE: I have *never* shared a room with *anyone*.
             My visitors have always been
             Strictly come-and-go. *[Innuendo]*
             A shared room?
             It might as well be the grave.
             It's my idea of Hell.

MRS. G: I'll be back to supervise your move
             On Monday. Meantime, I advise you,
             Decide what you want to bring with you.
             A few photos, some trinkets.
             There isn't room for all this –

PENNY: Memorabilia. That's what it is.

MRS. G: Then perhaps a museum would like it.

De VERE: It is my life. Without it
             I'll be dead in a month.

MRS. G: From what you say, that's no big deal.
             I'll see myself out.

[She exits. De VERE gets up. He becomes slightly faint as he does so, but steadies himself. Deep breath.]

De VERE: I think we all need a nice cup of tea.
                I hope you're both happy with Earl Grey.

[He exits.]

WALTER: *[To PENNY.]* I know what you're thinking.
              It's out of the question.

PENNY: Why not? The squat is huge.
             There's lots of spare rooms
             On the second floor.

WALTER: Which he can't reach. Those stairs…

PENNY: Put a stair lift in –

WALTER: Which he will be too proud to use.

PENNY: I'd love to have a gay grandad.

WALTER: Didn't you hear? He isn't gay.
              He's in the closet.
              How will he deal with twenty raging queers
              Coming and going at all hours,
              Tripping half the time on LSD?

[De VERE enters again with tea things on a tray. Over the

De VERE: Are you talking about money?
             Only people who don't have any
             Talk about money.

WALTER: No, Mr de Vere. I was talking about drugs.

PENNY: There are lots of drugs at the squat.
             Walter thinks you won't approve.

WALTER: I don't care if he approves or not.

De VERE: *[Dreamily]* Drugs… That takes me back…
             Cocaine in the twenties…
             I used to go to dinner parties where
             Lady Diana Cooper served cocaine
             In salt cellars, one each end of the table.

PENNY: No!

De VERE: Oh yes. Everyone used it then.
             Queen Victoria I believe was very fond of it.

PENNY: No!

De VERE: I was introduced to it on the Western Front
             By Siegfried Sassoon,
             Before the Battle of the Somme.
             He had it sent from Harrods by his brother:

'A welcome present to friends on the Front'.
I remember there was morphine
In the kit as well. And a syringe.

[PENNY and WALTER are awe-struck, their jaws dropped.]

Of course cocaine's a godsend at an orgy.
Greatly enhances the prowess.
Barbara Cartland gave the most marvel-
    lous parties,
Orgies in all but name –
Full of naked men and dope.
Ivor and Noël came often.

WALTER: *[To PENNY:]* And this man isn't gay?!

PENNY: Ivor?

De VERE: Ivor Novello. Before your time.
            And Noël Coward. He died some months
                ago.
            We sent each other cards for forty years
            At Christmas time. I always wrote
            'Happy Birthday to you' on his.

[Blank looks.]

Noël? Christmas?
I used to call him the first Noël.
And of course he was. Incomparable.

49

WALTER: He was an uptight closet queen,
            A reactionary and a bigot.

De VERE: Noël never concerned himself
            With politics. He was an artist.

WALTER: A reactionary hack.
            Maids in uniform, French windows,
            Anyone for tennis –

De VERE: Artists are neither Right nor Left,
            Artists are Above.
            He was my friend, and very kind;
            I'd be obliged, Mr. Craig,
            If you would respect my feelings
            – Which, by the by, are entirely private.

WALTER: *[About to explode]* Mr. de Vere –

De VERE: *[Bland, polite, gimlet-eyed]* Yes, Mr Craig?

WALTER: *[Deflates]* I – you – nothing…

PENNY: This is lovely tea.
            [To WALTER:] Let it go. He wouldn't
                understand.
            [To De VERE:] Will you be all right?

WALTER: Respect, respect. All we hear
            Is demands for respect;

Respect the traditions,
Respect our good intentions,
Respect your elders and betters,
Respect the feelings of others.
We are paralysed with respect.

PENNY: We ought to go.

De VERE: I am entirely recovered,
           Thank you, Mr Dreadful.

PENNY: In that case we will go.
           There's several blocks
           We still have to leaflet.

De VERE: I understand. Your public, too, awaits.

WALTER: We could come and help you pack on
             Sunday.
           Help you chuck things out.

[Indicating gramophone –]

           That thing might be worth some money.

De VERE: *[Bristling]* Thank you, Mr Craig,
           That won't be necessary.

PENNY: He's going to barricade himself in,

Remember? *[To de VERE:]* You are, arncha?

It'll be very dramatic. I can't wait.

De VERE: Goodbye, Mr. Dreadful; goodbye, Mr Craig.

You must be going.

[He shoos them out.]

Aria

De VERE: What can I do?
Have I the strength left to fight?
Every day it gets more difficult
To be Valentine de Vere.
The stairs get steeper,
The shops recede into the distance,
The legs get weaker.

[He fondly strokes the gramophone.]

'Might be worth some money' – Ha!
The store of all my reputation,
My talent,
My memories,
My money,
My life.
No, I will not fade,
Or go without a fight,

While there is breath in me –
A door to lock, a key to turn.
I will stand
As long as I can stand.
I will stand here,
The candle will blaze
Before it gutters
And splutters
And fades to nothing.
Here I have lived,
Here I will die.

[He views his own performance. Ironic.]

Not bad, not bad.
The local press will love it.

[Slow fade to –]

BLACKOUT

Scene Two

[Outside the flat. WALTER and PENNY arguing.]

WALTER: How can we?

PENNY: He won't be any trouble –

WALTER: What do you mean?
           He'll be nothing *but* trouble.
           Look how *old* he is.

PENNY: How can you be so ageist?
           You of all people.

WALTER: I don't mean it like that.
           But he is. Old.
           He has blackouts, he falls.

PENNY: If he falls, we pick him up.

WALTER: If we're there at the time.

PENNY: There's always *someone* there.
           It's a squat, for Chrissake,
           There's never less than fifteen people.
           Always someone still in bed.

WALTER: Screwing or stoned.
           I wouldn't trust a frail old man

With any of them.

PENNY: It's better than an old folks' home,
Full of straights who smell of pee.

WALTER: He'll smell of pee.

PENNY: Rubbish. Didn't you smell the perfume?

WALTER: Covering the smell of pee.

PENNY: We must have him.
He's our history, our roots,
We need him to remind us who we are.

WALTER: We are struggle, we are revolution,
With our sisters in Liberation,
With our black brothers in Power.
We are not Noël and Ivor
And Barbara fucking Cartland.

PENNY: We have a duty to care for our own –

WALTER: We have a duty to change society,
Not to apply a sticking plaster to it.

PENNY: I remember at one of the weekly meetings,
They proposed a fighting fund
For gay men to contest entrapment cases
For cottage and soliciting offences,

To pay for legal fees and fines –
But you opposed it.

WALTER: Too right I did.
           We should be making life worse
           Not better for the ordinary gay.
           That's the only way to stir them up.
           We need to make them so mad
           That they riot in the street.
           We need to have our own Stonewall.
           Paying legal fees is pissing cash away
           For nothing.
           Is Valentine going to advance the revolution?

PENNY: Not rotting in an old folks' home, he
               ain't.

WALTER: He's simply an irrelevance.
           There are better ways to fund rebellion.

PENNY: Oh, you fucking hypocrite!
           Who has more money
           Than he can piss away?
           Who gets his Daddy's dividends
           From oil and exploitation?
           You could pay for all the courts in London.
           You could buy a flat for Valentine,
           Out of your small change –

WALTER: OK, OK, I'll buy him a fucking flat!

PENNY: Except it will not give him what he needs.
           Care. Love. Attention.
           He'll set fire to it one day,
           And still be taken into care.
           He needs the commune.
           He needs us.

WALTER: The others will never agree.

PENNY: How do you know?
           Oh yes, people always do what you want,
           Don't they?
           Oh, the entitlement of the rich
           And spoilt!
           If you're so sure, put it to the test.
           Take it to the house meeting,
           See what they say.
           And I'll speak up for Valentine.

WALTER: Hey, what's happened to you?
           When did you get so mouthy
           All of a sudden?

PENNY: When I saw what a heartless shit
           I was going with.

WALTER: *[Weary]* OK, OK.
           Put it to the others in the house.

PENNY: And you'll abide by what they say?

WALTER: I suppose so.

PENNY: *[Hugging him:]* You see? That wasn't so
             hard, was it?

Duet

[Simultaneously]

WALTER: A frail old man – who needs him?
             They'll never take him,
             He'll be in the way.
             What a drag!
             Nothing but demands,
             Nothing but needs.
             We are young, we are strong.
             We must get on with the struggle –
             We haven't time to care
             For a frail old man.

PENNY: What a gorgeous queen! –
             They'll love him!
             How I can see him –
             He'll be holding court
             In no time.
             We can learn from him,
             See how we were.
             He's our past, he's our roots,
             And he's funny –
             Camp as Christmas.

And we need him there –

PENNY: Such a strong –

WALTER: Such a frail –

BOTH: Old man.

WALTER: Just a burden –

PENNY: A survivor –

WALTER: We must leave him.

PENNY: To be cherished.

WALTER: Life's too short –

PENNY: Life's too short –

WALTER: To wallow in the past.

PENNY: We need to know our past.

WALTER: Cut out the dead wood –

PENNY: Take inspiration –

WALTER/PENNY: From the past.

BOTH: Let the commune decide!

CROSSFADE TO –

Scene Three

[Inside de VERE's flat. He has put his clothes rack – minus clothes – and other furniture against the door. Only the gramophone is not pressed into service. He stand leaning against it in an attitude of defiance. The barricade is rather pathetic. A peremptory knock. We can also see MRS GOOD-HART outside at the door.]

MRS GOODHART: Mr de Vere... Mr de Vere...
It's Mrs Goodhart here.
You must stop being childish.
You cannot fight social services.
We know best –
It's for your own good.

[A pause. De VERE doesn't move.]

There's no point in this.
I have the police here, *[She indicates off-stage.]*
And a warrant to enter.
In a few moments I shall ask them
To break the door down.

[Another pause. Another silence.]

I shall ask the officer
To effect an entry
On a count of five.

Ready, officer?

[Another pause.]

I really do not want to do this,
Mr de Vere.
I do not want to damage Council property.

De VERE: And my property? What of that?
My records and my pictures and my costumes?

MRS. G: Those too, of course.

[Pause.]

A count of five…
One… Two… Three…

[PENNY and WALTER rush in.]

PENNY: *[Very dramatic]* Halt. Cease. Desist.

WALTER: Hold that policeman!

PENNY: In my dreams.

[WALTER produces two important looking pieces of paper.]

WALTER: I have here an affidavit –

A commitment made by Penny here
And me, to take care
Of Mr de Vere
In the Pink Poplar commune.
It was drawn up by Sir David Napley.
He is Jeremy Thorpe's solicitor
And knows my father.
He's much concerned with human rights
And miscarriages of justice.

PENNY: Mr de Vere, Mr de Vere,
             It's us. We've come to collect you
             And take you to the commune.
             You're in, doll.

De VERE: But what if I don't want
             To live in any commune?

PENNY: Don't be an annoying old faggot.
             You can come with us
             Or go and rot in the Cedars.
             Take your pick.
             Now let us in.
             Please –

WALTER: Please –

BOTH: Please!

[De VERE hesitates a long moment, then moves the coat rack

out of the way. He unlocks the door. PENNY and WALTER
push through. They clear a space, so MRS GOODHART can
follow.]

PENNY: *[To De VERE:]* What are you doing
              standing there?
            You'll do your legs no good.
            Go and sit down.

[De VERE does so. He is tired from the effort of defiance,
rather shrunken.]

MRS. G: *[Reading the paper:]*
            I'm afraid this will do you
            No good at all.
            It needs to be a relative,
            Or someone with a power of attorney.
            This undertaking isn't worth
            The paper that it's written on.
            The doctor's commitment still stands.
            I will call the policeman in
            To assist me.

WALTER: *[Another flourish:]* I also have here
            A Lasting Power of Attorney,
            Which Mr de Vere has only to sign,
            And we will be jointly and severally
            Entitled to take Mr de Vere –

De VERE: Into custody.

PENNY: Will you stop this? We're trying to help you.
            You're being very ungracious.

WALTER: Otherwise, I also have
            A statutory declaration,
            In which Mr de Vere
            Nominates me and/or Penny
            As next of kin.
            This too will entitle us
            To snatch him from your clutches.

PENNY: *[To MRS GOODHART:]* You can be the
               witness if you like –
            Like the matron of honour at a wedding.

De VERE: And do I have no say in this?

PENNY: Of course you have a choice.
            Next of kin or power of attorney.
            Walter's so clever at that kind of thing.

WALTER: Or go to the Cedars.

De VERE: When you are old the walls close in.
            The choices shrink,
            The pathways get more narrow.

PENNY: And you can bring all your lovely things,
            Play us your records,
            Tell us all your stories.

De VERE: I won't have to – sleep with anyone,
             Will I? *[He shudders.]*

PENNY: They'll be throwing themselves at you
             But you can always say No.
             [Sotto voce] Though that's not very polite.

WALTER: There's the sorting room at the back.
             It has running water.
             I thought we could turn it into a granny flat.

PENNY: Granny flat be buggered –
             The Star Dressing Room and Trailer!

WALTER: Whatever –

PENNY: *[To de VERE:]* Plus of course we'll cook
                 for you.
             It's all macrobiotic, of course,
             And ever so healthy.

De VERE: *[Pained]* Too kind.
             I think I'd find baked beans
             So much more convenient.

WALTER: You can have one of the new ovens –
             A microwave. We'll import one
             From America, they're the latest thing.

De VERE: What is a 'microwave'?

WALTER: It heats the dish by agitating the electrons.

PENNY: Sort of makes your shepherd's pie do the
            shimmy.

De VERE: Now that I would like to see.

MRS. G: Of course I shall have to see the commune;
            There are certain standards to observe,
            Cleanliness and safety.

PENNY: What do you take us for?

WALTER: We're not all hippies.

MRS. G: Then there's the question of drugs —

PENNY: *[To MRS GOODHART:]* You can't have
            any.
            [To de VERE:] We'll see about you.

De VERE: *[Genuine distress:]* I don't know what to do.
            I don't want to be
            In anybody's way.
            I always swore I wouldn't be a burden.

WALTER: I can assure you
            We will not allow you to become a burden.

PENNY: No. We'll have you put down if you start

to whinge.

De VERE: *[Starting to relent:]* I hope you would.

PENNY: Tell you what: we'll choke you
To death with your ostrich feathers.

De VERE: I shall insist that you all come to tea
Every Sunday afternoon –
Earl Grey in the Clarice Cliff,
And cucumber sandwiches.

PENNY: Cucumber sandwiches repeat on me.
I said, CUCUMBER SANDWICHES
REPEAT ON ME!

[He falls about at his own joke. WALTER glares.]

De VERE: You must come too, Mrs G.
You've been arguing with me
And bossing me about so long,
You feel like family.

MRS. G: You'll have to sign one of these first
Before we can release you.
You don't get away that easily.

WALTER: Attorney?

PENNY: Or next of kin?

[They dangle the papers before his eyes.]

BOTH: Which is it to be?

De VERE: Eeny – meeny – miney – mo –

[He closes his eyes and chooses one. PENNY looks at which one he's chosen.]

PENNY: Daddy!!! *[He rushes into De VERE's arms.]*

WALTER: We need a witness –

MRS. G: I'll be honoured. *[She signs.]*
               But I'll still need monthly visits
               And regular reports.

PENNY: Don't worry. We'll visit you.
               [To De VERE, confidential:]
               She's such a poor old soul,
               Doesn't see many people.
               Here! You'd best get everything packed.

De VERE: It already is.

PENNY: So you were going to move all along?
               You sly old –

De VERE: Sometimes one must surrender
               To the hand of Fate.

PENNY: I bet you've surrendered
            To some hands in your time.

De VERE: Don't be vulgar, Mr Dreadful.

PENNY: I apologise, Mr de Vere.

WALTER: Stop the double act, you two.
            The others will be here in fifteen minutes.

De VERE: Others?

WALTER: From the commune.
            We have volunteers to help.
            You don't think we're going to move
            All this trash ourselves – only joking! –
            These priceless antiques ourselves?

PENNY: Don't talk about my grandfather that way.

De VERE: I don't mind being an antique,
            As long as I am priceless.

PENNY: We'd better hurry,
            You'll need a quick rehearsal.

De VERE: Rehearsal?

PENNY: For the children's party.
            You're the main entertainment,

You're on at four o'clock.
Did you know we've got an old Joanna?
Though when those postmen found the
    time to play
I've no idea.
But Kitty Honour-Keyes
Is training as a concert pianist –
You should vada the martinis on that one.

De VERE: Vada the martinis!
I haven't heard that for thirty years.

PENNY: So get your arse in gear.

De VERE: I don't know about that.
I don't know if I'm suitable –
My material, I mean.

PENNY: Come off it, this is 1973.
Oz has had a Schoolkids' Issue,
Written and produced by teenagers,
Up in court as a dirty magazine.
Kids today, they've seen it all.
Done it too, more like.
To them you'll be as naughty
As Enid Blyton.
Now hurry up.
I got to iron your costume too,
Before you make your entrance.
They'll love you.

De VERE: I've always enjoyed a warm hand on my
             entrance.

*[He rummages in a box and produces the special scotch. A
search only produces one mug. He pours, takes a sip:]*

De VERE: To pastures new!

*[He passes the mug to MRS GOODHART, who takes a swig
and coughs. It goes to WALTER then PENNY. They sing 'To
Pastures New' in a round.]*

De VERE: *[To PENNY:]* Go on, you can have a
             swig.
             I don't think Mr Chevalier would mind.
             Besides, he's dead, and me – I'm alive!

WALTER: To change!

PENNY: To love!

MRS. G: To life!

De VERE: To life! *[With wonder:]* I'm alive!

BLACKOUT

INTERLUDE:

[Instrumental music creating the excitement and bustle of a children's party.]

[Front of stage, PENNY drags on the clothes rack we saw in de VERE's flat. WALTER brings a small table with a mirror and some make-up on it, and a chair. De VERE has removed his top, and has a towel round his neck. He is transforming himself into VICKY the GRUMPY OLD QUEEN. He is back on his home territory and completely in control. He sits at the table, applying some eyeliner, then some pale lipstick.]

PENNY: *[As he drags on the clothes rack:]*
           You'd better get a move on.

WALTER: *[As he brings the table on:]*
           Yeah, it's nearly ten to four.

PENNY: Just listen to those kids!

De VERE: Thank you, Mr. Craig.

WALTER: *[Anxious]* Is there anything else I can do?

De VERE: Terrify those tots into some kind of order.
           Tell them what happened to the Trotskyites
           At the fifteenth party congress.

WALTER: Gotcha! *[He exits busy, happy.]*

PENNY: *[Looking through the frocks:]*
             What did happen at the fifteenth –
                whatsit?

De VERE: How should I know?
             I'm sure something ghastly did.

[He shoos PENNY away from frocks.]

             We won't need any of that.
             Character, you understand,
             Is in the stance, and in the look,
             And in the voice.
             Just the shawl, please.

[PENNY brings it.]

             And two safety pins.
             Always carry safety pins.
             We'll make a dresser of you yet.

*[He stands and puts the shawl around his shoulders. PENNY
brings the pins and starts fussing to fix them.]*

De VERE: I can do that.
             Now where's the tea-towel?

PENNY: What do you want a tea-towel for?

De VERE: I assume that even hippies

Have to dry the dishes from time to time.
Mr Craig said he'd provide –
Ah, there it is.

[He puts the tea-towel over his head. PENNY pushes the table offstage.]

The sugar bowl, please.

PENNY: Sugar bowl?

De VERE: The *crown*. It's hanging on the end.

PENNY: This one?

De VERE: The very same.
Don't dent it, please, it's Georgian.

[De VERE takes the sugar bowl and puts it, inverted, on his head, over the tea-towel, and ties it under his chin.]

PENNY: Is that all there is to it?
A sugar bowl, a tea-towel, and a shawl?

De VERE: And – talent!

[He strikes a pose. Suddenly he has become VICTORIA.]

PENNY: Blimey! How do you do that?

De VERE: Trade secret. How do I look?

PENNY: Every inch a queen.

[He gives a deep curtsey as de VERE sweeps forward to the footlights.]

Scene Four

[The party. Noise of children. De VERE quells them with a look. Over the intro to the song, PENNY pushes the costume rack to the side. The lights have dimmed to give de VERE the sole and complete focus. Piano Introduction:]

De VERE: You see me with me orb
               And me sceptre in me hand –

               [Spoken:] It's a sceptre! Filthy minds!

               You see me with me orb
               And me sceptre in me hand;
               Me sceptre's only kept to stir me tea with;
               I keep you on your toes
               By looking down me nose –
               People say I'm not the gayest gal to be with!

               [Spoken:] And so they call me –

               Vicky the grumpy old queen;
               Grumpy and frumpy as crimp-er-lene.
               When I think of all yer sins,
               I shake me head and wobble me chins –

[Does so with a sound like a turkey.]

               If you talk to me, you must keep it clean;

Cos I'm Vicky – Vicky, the grumpy old
    queen.
As I remarked to me aide de camp –

[Spoken:] A bit more aid and a bit less
camp, if you don't mind!

As I remarked to me aide de camp,
'Look at me on the postage stamp!
They've got me left side, not me right side,
They might at least have shown me bright
    side.'
He said, 'You should be full of cheer,
Not grim and glum and so austere –
Cos everyone licks you on the rear,
Vicky, you grumpy old queen.'

[Spoken:] We were not amused.

I'm Vicky the grumpy old queen,
Wrapped like a parcel in bombazine.
Sons and grandsons in their dozens,
All of Europe's kings me cousins;
We lost a few to the guillotine,
But not Vicky the grumpy old queen.
I plunged in mourning when Albert died,
But soon John Brown was at me side.
He kept me as busy as I could be,
Tossing his caber for all to see.
I told protesters, 'Don't be silly;

He's not me hubby, he's me ghillie;
And who else should take me up the Dilly?'
I'm Vicky the grumpy old queen.

[Spoken:] Oh yes, he's had me up the
Dilly more times than I've had hot ban-
quets. Mind you, he's not a patch on
Albert, my dear husband. Albert was an
exhibitionist. In fact, he was a Great
Exhibitionist. Built a crystal palace, and
all so he could name a football team. I'll
never forget when he took me to see it in
Hyde Park. I said, Albert, what a magnifi-
cent erection. And the Palace isn't bad
either.

I'm Vicky the grumpy old queen,
Been on the throne since sweet eighteen –

[Spoken:] That's nearly fifteen years –
[A defiant look:] – It's true! The lighting
here is cruelly deceptive. Fifteen years I've
been sat on that throne. Me constipation's
something chronic. Nothing but a
plunger can shift it.

I'm Vicky the grumpy old queen,
Been on the throne since sweet eighteen.
When Albert came it was love at first sight;
On his knees he was just my height.

After he'd begun to propose,
He said, 'I've a secret I must disclose;
I've got a ring, and I've got a spare –
It's kept quite safe – you won't guess
    where';
I never knew rings could be kept Down
    There –
I said, 'Albert, you're rather obscene';
I'm Vicky the grumpy old queen.
I'm Vicky the grumpy old queen
Rich as Croesus and fearfully mean
I own the world – the map's all pink!

[Spoken:] Pink is sooo gay!

I own the world – the map's all pink!
Everything and the kitchen sink;
I'm laden from Aden to Aberdeen.
I'm Vicky, the grumpy old Queen.
I'm Vicky, the grumpy old Queen.
Try to cross me, I'll make a scene.
Seen Prime Ministers come and go;
They all have got the old heave-ho –
I just flush them down the latrine…

[Spoken:] Otherwise known as the House
of Lords.

… I'm Vicky the grumpy old Queen
I had Mr Gladstone and Mr Disraeli,

A terrible flirt who teased me daily.
He said to me gaily, 'Call me Dizzy',
Which put me in the most frightful tizzy.
'If I call you Dizzy,' I told him, 'Laddie,
I'll have to call Mr Gladstone, Gladdie,
Or else he'll be so green,
And though I'm frightfully keen,
I won't be known as the Dizzy Queen,
When I'm Vicky the grumpy old queen.
I'm Vicky the grumpy old Queen,
And though you think I'm a has-been,
I'm still all round you, ask any historian,
My attitudes live and they're quite dino-
  saurian.
Better watch out for those values Victorian,
They're everywhere still to be seen,
Thanks to Vicky – I'm so tricky –
Vicky – call me picky –
Vic – don't take the Mickey –
Vicky the grumpy old queen.

[APPLAUSE. BOW.

FADE TO BLACKOUT.

END]

A Gay Century: 12

1982: After Sefton

A Love Story

For Robert Ely

To Leda Kosmachevskaya,
her husband,
and her husband's husband

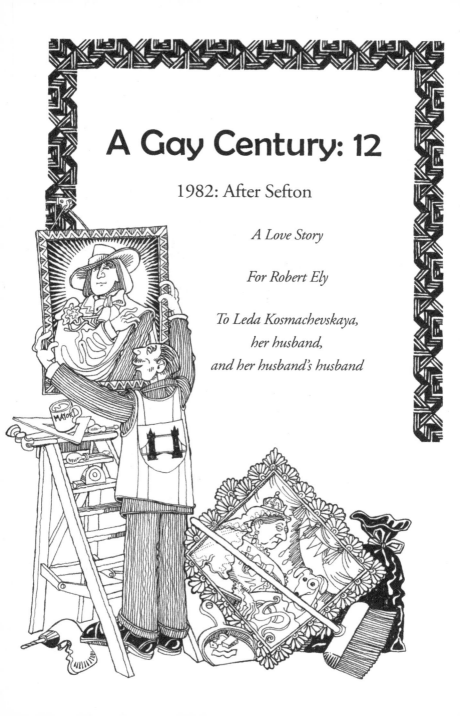

Above: *1982 Hyde Park bombing – The Dead Horses* [Daily Mail]
Below: *1982 Regent's Park Bombing – Memorial*

Introduction

1981–82 was a busy year for the IRA, and a bloody year for Londoners. In October '81, Chelsea Barracks was bombed, killing two and injuring 39. It was closely followed by a car bomb in Dulwich and one in a Wimpey Bar in Oxford Street, which killed the man trying to defuse it. A month later there was one at the barracks in Woolwich.

All these, bad as they were, paled before the events of 20th July, 1982, when two bombs exploded within two hours of each other. The first was at Hyde Park Barracks, in a column going off to the Trooping of the Colour, and the second in Regent's Park, under the bandstand. The first was remarkable for the carnage among the horses of the Blues and Royals. Three soldiers were killed, and seven horses. One horse, Sefton, struggled for life dramatically under the blaze of tabloid spotlights. In Regent's Park, two hours later, six bandsmen of the Royal Green Jackets were killed outright and 24 injured, one fatally, along with a dozen or so concert spectators.

What was remarkable at the time was the intense focus on the fate of the horses, especially Sefton, which elbowed out more human concerns about the wounded and dead. As the libretto says, we are a nation of animal-lovers, not soldier-lovers. There are monuments to the dead in both Regent's Park and Hyde Park; but if you search 'IRA bombings' on the internet, the overwhelming majority of pictures are not of people, but of Sefton and the other horses. Sefton had an extraordinary medical ordeal. He had a severed jugular vein, an eye out, and 34 wounds from the 4-inch nails that ripped through him. Eight hours of surgery followed – there had never been such complex operations on a horse. Cards and gifts and donations of over £600,000 flowed in, which were enough for a new surgical wing at the Royal Veterinary College. Numerous TV appearances followed, and a Horse of the Year award.

We the public knew little about the individual soldiers who died or were injured, and the reaction of their families and friends. However, it is a statistical probability that one of them was gay or bisexual. I have always resisted the 'heteronormative' narrative imposed on national calamity. It was a by-word among the gay community that one of those who went to the aid of other passengers in the disastrous fire at Kings Cross Underground station in 1987 [a hospital nurse called, if I remember rightly, Paul] was gay. He was a hero, and he was airbrushed. Similarly, when the *Marchioness* pleasure boat was hit and capsized in the Thames in 1989, none of the coverage mentioned the sexuality of the 51 victims.

The Marchioness was hosting a party, organised by Jonathan Phang for his partner Antonio de Vasconcellos's 26th birthday. They ran a modelling agency together. The boat was full of beautiful, gilded, mostly gay people. The DJ, who was one of the drowned, was Jamie Peters, younger brother of the better-known Colin Peters, a popular gay DJ. The account of the bungled postmortems, mis-identifications and cover-ups in the face of the persistent distress and anger of families and friends is shaming. But nowhere on Wikipedia to this day is there any mention that this was, to all intents and purposes, a gay party, and a gay tragedy.

This invisibility is compounded by the self-imposed invisibility of gay people themselves, encouraged by a society which punishes openness. So many historic lives of lesbians and gay men are sketchy either because of the caution of those who do not wish to be 'found out', who destroy or fail to keep letters, diaries etc.; or because of the wilful destruction of such material by family and 'well-meaning' friends who wish to create an 'unsullied' reputation for their subject.[4]

I mention all this, because the closet allows no hint of the emotional depths experienced by gay men, and nowhere is this truer than in the Armed Forces. In the 1950s and 60s, homosexual rights organisers were advising their members, 'don't keep diaries, or letters, or even Christmas cards.' This was doubly urgent if you were in the Army or Navy, and remained so until the twenty-first century. This year [2020] we are celebrating the twentieth anniversary of the decriminalisation of same-sex relationships in the Forces, but even since then there have been

---

[4] A classic instance of this is the lyricist, Lorenz Hart, creative partner of Richard Rodgers, whose papers were systematically burned by Rodgers and his sister-in-law, Dorothy, to prevent the truth emerging. Even 45 years after his death, when Dorothy was editing the complete lyrics, there are no acknowledgments of homosexuality, only vague references to loneliness, emotional inadequacy, and the self-consciousness of being short and ugly. For years I've had in mind an anthology show about the real crucifixion of Lorenz Hart entitled *Doc Bender's Bum Boy Revue*, although I doubt if the puritan and hagiographic Rodgers estate would countenance the use of Richard's music to such unholy purposes for a moment.

plenty of unreconstructed homophobes who have made life difficult for Queer forces personnel and their same-sex partners. It was still possible for people to be dismissed for 'conduct prejudicial to good order and discipline', where homosexuality was the unspoken underlying cause of dismissal. Thankfully that behaviour is now a thing of the past – we hope.

My writing partner, Robert Ely, was one of those who suffered under the old order. He had been a Warrant Officer, 1st Class, and a Bandmaster in the Parachute Regiment. Outed in 1986, he was dishonourably discharged, losing all his medals, his references and his pension in the process. In response he founded the organisation *Rank Outsiders* and gave evidence to a Parliamentary Select Committee, which still held in 1991 that homosexuals in the ranks were a threat to good order and discipline. Perhaps unwisely, he accepted a niggardly settlement with the Ministry of Defence which in no way compensated him for the emotional and financial damage done to him. He is still trying to get a better deal.

I wanted this part of the cycle to reflect his harrowing experience. Therefore I've combined it with my own hobbyhorse about the damaging and self-reinforcing phenomenon of invisibility. I have no direct experience of being gay in the armed forces, and I've never talked to anyone about it in any detail. Therefore I was delighted to have the endorsement of both Robert and of another ex-Forces man, Patrick Lyster-Todd [navy], who were two of the quartet which took the Government to the European Court of Human Rights to force change. It seems that I have nailed both the emotional cost and the petty details of Military Police investigation simply by imagining it. People who think docu-drama is inherently superior because based on 'real life', please note.

At the heart of this piece is an ironic contradiction, where exposure by enforced dismissal is paradoxically a liberating experience. The central character is in an intense relationship with a young bandsman who dies in Regent's Park. By conforming to the army code, he cannot mourn the loss of his great love, because that love cannot exist. By being forced out, he gains the space for his feelings and finds a way to compensate for the betrayal of his partner which his denials amounted to. The most oppressive thing which happens to Robert Duggan is also the most liberating.

Peter Scott-Presland
29 March 2022

CAST

CORPORAL ROBERT DUGGAN: Baritone
35, a cornet player, Royal Marine Band. Profoundly cautious, slow to show emotion. In the present [2001], when he talks to the audience, he is in his early sixties.

BANDSMAN ADAM FRASER: Tenor
19, a flute player in the Royal Green Jackets Band, a cheerful Jack-the-Lad.

MAJOR WILDER: Bass
Early 50s. Royal Military Police, Special Investigation Branch. Professionally impassive, devious, smart. Nearing retirement.

SERGEANT TROSSLEY: Baritone
35, a trombone player, Royal Marine Band. A jovial man who likes his beer. An old and close friend of Duggan [Doubles as a non-singing Priest, possibly offstage.]

[All characters are fictional.]

SETTING

July 1982 and 2001

Open; various military locations.

INSTRUMENTS

Flute, cornet, trombone.

AFTER SEFTON

Scene One

[1982 – An interrogation. ROBERT DUGGAN is seated at a table. A bag [containing letters] is nearby. MAJOR WILDER stands; he has a letter in his hand. Both men are in uniform.]

WILDER: *[Showing DUGGAN the letter:]* Is this your handwriting?

DUGGAN: Yes…

WILDER: *[Reading:]* 'I miss you so much. I live for the times
We can snatch together.'
What does that mean?

DUGGAN: We were friends.

WILDER: Good friends?

DUGGAN: Yes…

WILDER: Intimate friends?

DUGGAN: I suppose so…

WILDER: Sharing-a-bed, doing-the-dirty friends?

DUGGAN: No!
           Where did you get that letter?

WILDER: It's not the only one.
           There were several in his locker.

DUGGAN: *[To himself:]* Of all the stupid –

WILDER: What did you say?

DUGGAN: Nothing.

WILDER: Let's start again.
           Where did you meet him?

Scene Two

[Lights change. DUGGAN steps out to the audience – he picks up a drink.]

DUGGAN: It was the Pig and Whistle,
                  Saturday lunchtime.
                  I don't know if you remember it.
                  In a mews in Belgravia.
                  White wash walls, beer garden,
                  Jam-packed on a nice warm day,
                  Or spilling onto the street.
                  It was one of those pubs,
                  Only gay one day a week.
                  Like the Markham in the King's Road.

[ADAM FRASER wanders in, obviously new, beer in hand.]

DUGGAN: He had the bluest eyes.

[FRASER sees DUGGAN and smiles.]

DUGGAN: *[To audience:]* I was on holiday.
                  I'd had a couple, I was bold.
                  Anyone who saw me in the Pig and Whistle
                  From the Commando –
                  Well, what was *he* doing there anyway?
                  I was careful.
                  I never went to the gay pub in Portsmouth.

[He approaches FRASER.]

<blockquote>Looking for someone?</blockquote>

FRASER: *[Smiling]* Maybe...

DUGGAN: Anyone in particular?

FRASER: That depends...

DUGGAN: *[To audience:]* He was so relaxed,
At ease within his skin.
I never would have guessed.

FRASER: Is it always this busy?

DUGGAN: *[To FRASER:]* Later it will be dead.
They'll all move on to the King's Road.
To the Markham,
Or to Habitat for coffee, cake – and
    cruising...

DUGGAN: *[To audience:]* I don't know why I said that.
I don't know how I dared.
Adam gave me confidence,
He looked so self-assured,
It must have rubbed off onto me.
Some of it.

FRASER: Where's Habitat? I don't know London well.

DUGGAN: First-time visitor?

FRASER: Not a visitor, but not been here long.

DUGGAN: Habitat's in the King's Road too.

FRASER: Seems everything's in the King's Road,
            Everything you could want.

DUGGAN: It is on a Saturday afternoon.

FRASER: Will you be in the King's Road too?

DUGGAN: I could be.

            [To audience] I was falling,
            Falling deep into his eyes.
            I was starting to get hard,
            I hoped it didn't show
            Through my tracksuit bottoms.

FRASER: *[Seeing the erection, with amusement:]*
            If I persuaded you?

DUGGAN: *[To audience:]* He already had.

[FRASER exits – taking DUGGAN's drink.]

BLACKOUT

Scene Three

[HABITAT coffee shop on the top floor of the store. A cloth-covered table with a flower in a vase. FRASER and DUGGAN are sat having coffee.]

FRASER: What do you do?

DUGGAN: *[Confused]* Do?

FRASER: For a living?
             What did you think I meant?

DUGGAN: *[Not sure whether to tell the truth.]*
             I'm from Portsmouth.

FRASER: Navy?

DUGGAN: Sort of –
             [To audience:] How could I be so open?
             It went against all my instincts.

FRASER: *[Boastful]* I'm a bandsman –
             Royal Green Jackets.

DUGGAN: Not so loud!

FRASER: It's no big deal these days.

DUGGAN: How long have you been in the Black Mafia?

FRASER: You know the Royals then?

DUGGAN: How long?

FRASER: Nine months.

DUGGAN: You have a lot to learn.
            Take my advice, be very careful.
            People are still thrown out
            For being gay.

FRASER: All my colleagues know.

DUGGAN: It only takes a quarrel
            For one to turn against you.
            Or one to blackmail you
            Into having sex.
            Or one new squaddie
            Not so understanding.

[FRASER laughs. DUGGAN seizes his arm.]

DUGGAN: I'm serious. Take care.
            Protect your back.
            Never keep a diary,
            Never save a letter,
            Burn it if there's anything suggestive –
            If you tear it up,
            They can piece it together.

FRASER: Is that what you do?

DUGGAN: I never get letters.

FRASER: That's sad. *[Pause.]*
            Have you never had a boyfriend?

DUGGAN: No. I loved a boy at school, but –
            No.

FRASER: I had a boyfriend,
            But when I joined the army, he left me.
            He was a pacifist and a bit of a hippy.
            Now he's married to a florist.

            [Pause.]

            I miss having a boyfriend.

DUGGAN: Want another coffee?

[FRASER shakes his head. Pause.]

            Wanna come to Hyde Park with me?
            [Suggestive] We could go into the bushes.

FRASER: *[Alarmed]* Are you crazy?
            Who was going on about risks?
            Let's go to your hotel.

DUGGAN: They know me there.

[FRASER leans forward and kisses his hand before DUGGAN can withdraw.]

FRASER: *[Deeply suggestive]* Let's go to another
            hotel.

[Lights change. DUGGAN moves to the front, alone.]

DUGGAN: *[To audience:]* It was hopeless.
            I was helpless
            In the gaze of those melting eyes,
            In the feel of those moist red lips.

Scene Four

[Lights change. Interrogation once more. DUGGAN sits at the table.]

WILDER: When was this?

DUGGAN: Mrs Thatcher just got in.
            Nineteen seventy nine.
            Summer.

WILDER: And nothing passed between you?

DUGGAN: Nothing. I'm not homosexual.

DUGGAN: *[To audience:]* I felt dreadful saying that.
            Like pissing on his grave.

WILDER: So you're not queer.

DUGGAN: No

WILDER: Just happened to be in a haunt of queers.

DUGGAN: I'm not queer!

WILDER: Maybe you just help them out
            When they're short-handed.

DUGGAN: It wasn't a gay pub.

WILDER: On a Saturday it was.

[Pause. WILDER gets another letter from the bag.]

             This is dated nineteen eighty-one –
             Two years later.

DUGGAN: We kept in touch.

WILDER: Where are his letters?

DUGGAN: What?

WILDER: His letters to you, where are they?
             We searched your locker – nothing.
             A bit one-sided, was it?
             Older man, younger man.
             Taking you for a ride, was he?

DUGGAN: I never keep letters.
             They don't seem important…

WILDER: [Another letter] This one is dated Christmas
             Nineteen-eighty.
             'My dearest Adam,
             I'm sitting alone in my room
             Writing this. Grannie is downstairs,
             Making pigs in blankets for tomorrow.
             I don't know why,
             We have far too much food anyway

For the two of us.
Tradition I suppose.
We have to have pigs in blankets.

I keep wanting to tell her
About our little secret,
But I don't think she could stand it
At her age. I'm all she has.
It would kill her.
'Our little secret'.
What little secret? *[Pause.]*

DUGGAN: I thought I was going to be posted
               To Northern Ireland.
               It could have been really dangerous.
               There's been so many bombs.

[WILDER carries on reading.]

WILDER: 'I'm only here for five days,
               But already it seems an age.
               I know we'll be together
               On my next leave in February.
               I can't tell you how much
               My heart swells with longing.
               Oh my dearest sweet boy,
               Without you, my life has
               No interest at all,
               No flavour at all.
               All the joy and colour has gone.'

[WILDER stops reading.]

        'My dearest sweet boy…'
        Is that what you call a friend?
        Even a very good friend?
        This is a love letter, admit it.

DUGGAN: No.

WILDER: Of course it bloody well is!
        Why do you go on denying it?
        There are others.
        There are many, many others.

[He goes to the bag and pulls out a fistful of letters. He reads lines from different letters at random]

        'My dearest darling' –
        'My one and only joy' –
        'Your skin is like the softest silk' –
        'You are the light of my life' –
        'Last night when we lay together' –

        What the hell are you playing at?

Scene Five

[Lights change again. DUGGAN to audience.]

DUGGAN: 'Last night, when we lay together…'
              I remember where I wrote that.
              Paddington Station.
              My skin was still glowing,
              I could feel your kisses on my back.
              I blushed as I wrote it.
              I was sure everyone could tell.
              How could anyone know so much happiness
              In a cheap knocking shop?
              It had to show in my face, in my eyes…

*[Lights change. A cheap hotel in Paddington. FRASER enters
to DUGGAN. He is stripped to the waist.]*

FRASER: …in a 'cheap knocking shop'?

DUGGAN: Well it was, wasn't it?
              You could take a room by the hour.

FRASER: But we had all night.
              And the next day. And night.

DUGGAN: I'd never let anyone do that before.

FRASER: *[To audience:]* It slipped in like it was
                  fated.

105

DUGGAN: It hurt at first...

FRASER: But I held you, and licked you,
            And kissed the hairs
            On the nape of your neck,
            Till you were relaxed –

DUGGAN: And we were one.
            That's how it seemed,
            We became a single person.
            I loved you so much.

FRASER: I loved you too.
            My angel!

DUGGAN: My life!

FRASER: I never want to be parted.
            I can't stand much more of this –
            The furtiveness, the fear –

DUGGAN: The fear is my fault –

BOTH: We will conquer fear.

[They kiss passionately.]

DUGGAN: It doesn't have to be for long,
            This life of yearning.
            I can be out in a year.

I will be thirty-six,
We can have over forty years together.

FRASER: No, fifty.

DUGGAN: More than half a lifetime.

FRASER: I can be out in two years –

DUGGAN: Two years? I'll be thirty-seven!
How can I stand the wait?

FRASER: Be patient, darling.
You'll get a job as a music teacher,
Find us both a flat to share –
Somewhere nice.

DUGGAN: Somewhere nice?
Anywhere is nice with you.
Anywhere without you is a hell,
A hell of loneliness and longing.

FRASER: I can join an orchestra or band –
Perhaps the BBC, it's full of poufs!

DUGGAN: I'm sure you're good enough.

FRASER: I'm pouf enough!
Maybe you can join them too?

DUGGAN: It would be good to play together…

FRASER: We're playing together now! *[Kiss.]*

DUGGAN: Not like that – be serious!

FRASER: Oh, I am, I am.
               You don't know how serious I am.

DUGGAN: I couldn't get an orchestra,
               I'm nowhere near as good as you.

[FRASER takes a ring off his finger. He grabs DUGGAN's hand and tries to put the ring on his marriage finger.]

FRASER: Here…
               This was my Grandad's.

[DUGGAN reacts as if it was red hot.]

DUGGAN: No. People will ask.
               I'll have to explain it.
               I'll have to lie.

FRASER: I never want to lie.

DUGGAN: You're different. I'm too old.

FRASER: All right, Grandpa.

[He puts the ring back on his finger, takes a chain with a cross on it from around his neck, and puts it round DUGGAN's.]

	You can explain this. Say you won it in a church raffle.

DUGGAN: That sounds ridiculous.

FRASER: OK, say you got it for being shagged
    rotten
By a member of the Black Mafia.
Tell them it's the wages of sin
And sin pays very well.

DUGGAN: Now you're being stupid.

FRASER: *[Serious]* It was from my mum.
She gave it me before she died.
I want you to feel me against your skin
Every moment of the day.

[Lights change.]

Scene Six

[Back to the interrogation. WILDER is offstage in shadow.]

WILDER: The postmark is Waterloo,
                Dated Fourth of June
                Nineteen-eighty two.

DUGGAN: I remember that so well.
                He slipped out of the room
                With one last look.
                We smiled. *[FRASER exits.]*
                I sat there on the rumpled bed,
                And looked around the faded peeling walls
                With patterns of forget-me-nots.
                I wondered when we'd meet again.
                No more leave till autumn –
                Military bands are always busy
                In the summer.
                Parks, bandstands, end of the pier.
                Kids with ice creams
                Playing soldiers;
                Older codgers dozing
                On the benches.
                A nice little earner,
                Sweating in the sun.
                I wrote down all my feelings,
                White hot from my heart.

WILDER: *[Reading]* 'I can feel your tongue in my

mouth,
Your teeth nibbling at my neck...'

DUGGAN: I had a fancy writing case,
           A gift from my mates
           On my thirtieth.
           It felt good to take it out,
           The Platignum pen,
           To hear it scratching
           On the Basildon Bond,
           The words shaping under the nib,
           Strong and sure with love.

WILDER: 'In the mirror I can see the marks
           On my shoulders where you held me.
           Your muscles were so firm,
           The biceps under the skin,
           Under a skin so soft.'

DUGGAN: I couldn't bear to dress.

WILDER: 'The marks will fade.
           The red will fade
           Under my clothes,
           Even while I go about
           The business of the world.
           I do not want to put my singlet on
           While I can see the marks
           And feel your presence.'
           Well? Well? *[Pause.]*

DUGGAN: Eventually I forced myself to dress,
            Paid the bill,
            Popped the letter in the letter box
            At Waterloo,
            On the way to Platform Five,
            And Portsmouth.
            [Exploding] All right,
            Have it your way.
            I only wanted to keep his name
            From publicity,
            Protect his family.
            [He collapses.]
            What does it matter now he's dead?

WILDER: It matters to those left behind.
            We must make examples
            Of rotten apples,
            For the other rotten apples
            Still lurking in the basket.

DUGGAN: For the sake of his family.
            They must remember him
            As they saw him, at his best.
            Why should they be told?
            Why should he be held up to scorn?
            'Adam Fraser, martyr to the IRA
            And screaming pansy.'

WILDER: Conduct prejudicial
            To good order and discipline.

Don't worry, we can't try
A soldier once he's dead.

DUGGAN: You would though, wouldn't you?
If you could.
Drag his name through the mud.

WILDER: I don't think so –
Wouldn't do the army any good,
Putting wrong ideas in people's heads.
We might get all the wrong type of recruits
For all the wrong reasons.

DUGGAN: *[To audience:]* I joined the Royal Marines
Because the men were more handsome,
And the uniforms more sexy.

WILDER: Try telling that to your Court Martial.
Can't see that going down very well.

DUGGAN: Court Martial?

WILDER: Your discharge hearing then.

DUGGAN: And Adam's name?

WILDER: Corporal, the hearing's confidential.
We're not monsters.
You can be represented.

DUGGAN: I don't need to be represented.
            My life is over.

WILDER: As you wish.

[Lights fade. DUGGAN slowly comes forward to address the audience.]

DUGGAN: There was no internet of course
            Not back then in nineteen eighty-two.
            Hard to remember now a time without it.
            There were letters… Only letters.

Scene Seven

[The Barracks. TROSSLEY rushes in; he carries a post-bag containing letters.]

TROSSLEY:	Been to the Postie And picked up the mail.
DUGGAN:	*[Eager]* Anything for me?
TROSSLEY:	*[Teasing]* Eager beaver, aren't we? Expecting something?
DUGGAN:	Might be –
TROSSLEY:	Meet someone on leave, did we?
DUGGAN:	None of your business.
TROSSLEY:	You did!
DUGGAN:	Give it here.
TROSSLEY:	Give what where?
DUGGAN:	My letter. I know you've got a letter for me.
TROSSLEY:	Might have –
DUGGAN:	Don't be such a prick.

115

TROSSLEY: Language!

DUGGAN: Give it here.

[TROSSLEY reaches in his bag, while he does so:]

TROSSLEY: I think there may be something here.
I seem to remember –

DUGGAN: Stop dragging it out.

TROSSLEY: Isn't this exciting? I feel like Santa Claus…

DUGGAN: Get on with it!

TROSSLEY: You must really be in love.

[He finds the letter and holds it out; snatches it away when DUGGAN goes to grab it.]

TROSSLEY: What's her name?

DUGGAN: What?

TROSSLEY: A fair exchange; one letter – one name.

DUGGAN: If you must know, it's my sister.

TROSSLEY: Is that all? Why so much excitement?

[Duggen searches for an excuse.]

DUGGAN: She's expecting a baby.

[TROSSLEY looks unconvinced.]

It could be any day now.

TROSSLEY: If the baby had arrived she would have
            called.

DUGGAN: She's in the Hebrides.

TROSSLEY: They have phones.

DUGGAN: The Outer Hebrides.

TROSSLEY: *[Sighing]* Well, if you won't, you won't.

[He gives DUGGAN the letter, reluctantly.]

Here you are... *uncle.*
You're no fun.

[He exits. DUGGAN tears open the letter and starts to read it excitedly.]

[FRASER appears in a spotlight on the opposite side of the stage.]

DUGGAN: My dearest, dearest darling,
            My sweet hot man…

FRASER: *[Joining in]* My sweet hot man –

FRASER: Even thinking of you as I write
            I get excited.
            My cock is hard,
            My Y-fronts wet with pre-cum.

DUGGAN: I go back over in my mind
            Our last weekend,
            Every moment –
            The lagers from the off-licence,
            The takeaway pizzas.

FRASER: I never wanted to get out of bed
            The whole weekend.

DUGGAN: Darling, I'm worried for you –

FRASER: If you're sent to the Falklands –

DUGGAN: If you're sent to Northern Ireland –

FRASER: The rumour is, they'll send in the Marines
            If it goes on for much longer.
            Those Argies are tougher
            Than people think.

DUGGAN: Danger on every street corner:
            Snipers, unexploded bombs.

FRASER: It could go on for months. Years.

DUGGAN: If anything were to happen...

FRASER: We could all be dragged in.

DUGGAN: What would I do then?

[Pause.]

FRASER: I'm quite excited.
            I've got my first band concert
            In Regent's Park, July
            The Twentieth.
            I get to do two solos –
            From 'Oliver' – by Lionel Bart.
            The arranger thinks that little Oliver
            Is worth a flute, all frail and wistful.
            I'll do my best to make you proud of me,
            Like I am proud of you.

DUGGAN: I am proud of you.

FRASER: So proud –

DUGGAN: So proud –

FRASER: So proud of you.

*[The music breaks off abruptly. In the silence, DUGGAN
takes a lighter out of his pocket, and sets fire to the letter. He
watches it burn.]*

DUGGAN: I leave no traces
                      But the traces in my heart.

Scene Eight

[Lights change. DUGGAN at the table with his writing set. He is writing back to FRASER.]

DUGGAN: My dear Angel,
            I am so nervous for you.
            Today is your big day.
            I know the bandstand well
            In Regent's Park,
            By the boating lake.
            I hope it's a fine day,
            And no wind
            To blow your music about.

[FRASER appears in his quarters. He is cleaning and preparing his dress uniform for the concert.]

FRASER: *[As he cleans his Sam Browne belt:]*
            I put the button stick
            Behind the buckle.
            Silvo Tarnish Guard,
            Metal polish wadding,
            And then a cloth.
            The jacket is just back
            From the cleaners,
            So I have no need.
            Nerves, I suppose,
            Displacement activity.
            I want it to be perfect.

I want to do you proud.

DUGGAN: I know you'll do me proud.
            I wish I could be there.

FRASER: I wish you could be here.

BOTH: To hear your/my solos.

[SPOTLIGHTS FADE TO BLACK]

Scene Nine

[Lights up abruptly. A clang of an alarm bell off stage. TROSSLEY and DUGGAN run in.]

DUGGAN: What's happened? What is it?

TROSSLEY: Haven't you heard? The IRA –
            Those bastards struck again.

DUGGAN: Where?

TROSSLEY: Knightsbridge Barracks,
            When the Blues and Royals were going for
            The changing of the guard.
            There's a general alert, we must muster.

DUGGAN: Any killed? How many killed?

TROSSLEY: Troopers? Three.
            I don't know about horses.

DUGGAN: Horses?

TROSSLEY: It's a bomb, stupid.
            Household cavalry –
            Changing of the guard –
            Course they got some horses.
            I'll take a quick look
            At the telly in the mess,

See if it's on the news.

[Exits fast.]

DUGGAN: It was on the telly.
             News flash.
             Seven horses killed,
             Or put out of their misery –
             The TV doesn't show that,
             Or the smell of burnt horse flesh
             Reeking in the nostrils;
             Or the dreadful screams that horses make
             When they are ripped open.
             One horse fighting for his life.
             Sefton. Nineteen years old –
             Chestnut – white flash
             Down the muzzle.
             Severed jugular, wounded in the eye,
             Flayed by four inch nails.
             They rushed him from Hyde Park
             Back to Barracks.
             Emergency operation.
             Ninety minutes.
             No-one thought that he'd survive.
             The nation held its breath,
             And forgot the troopers killed.
             We are animal lovers,
             Not squaddie lovers.

[TROSSLEY comes running back.]

TROSSLEY: There's been another bomb.

DUGGAN: Where?

TROSSLEY: Regent's Park,

[*DUGGAN almost collapses, speechless with horror.*]

TROSSLEY: At the bandstand.

BOTH: Royal Green Jackets.

TROSSLEY: How did you know that?

DUGGAN: *[Soft]* I have a friend –

TROSSLEY: Seven bandsmen killed,

DUGGAN: *[To himself:]* Maybe… Please God…

TROSSLEY: They were playing music from *Oliver!*
              When the bomb went off
              Underneath the bandstand.

[*The lighting fades on the periphery slowly, until the spot is only on DUGGAN*]

TROSSLEY: *[Spoken, only half seen in shadow:]* I mean,
                     it's less than two hours after the other
                     one. Already three dead, and now

another seven. Maybe more. All those
people standing round, or sitting in
deckchairs, listening to the music, then
blown off their feet as bits of men and
metal fly all around them.

The order is, we're confined to barracks,
fuck it, and you can see why, though
really it's just as likely there's a bomb
here somewhere, as another in the Park.

DUGGAN: *[Sung over TROSSLEY:]*
He must be one of them,
The Dead.
He was at the front,
Forward for his solo.
Sweating in his Rifle Green jacket
And his brushed forage cap.

TROSSLEY: *[Spoken]* I just want to get down there
and be with them and help somebody.

[Pause.]

[Explodes] I just want to KILL SOME-
THING.

*[After TROSSLEY's explosion, only the solo flute. Then the
solo flute is cut off abruptly in mid-phrase. They stand frozen,
silent. Lights return to normal.]*

126

TROSSLEY: Are you all right, mate?

DUGGAN: It's the shock, it's awful.

TROSSLEY: You look half-dead yourself.

DUGGAN: I'll be alright.

TROSSLEY: How well did you know him?
              This friend?

DUGGAN: Hardly at all.
              More an acquaintance.

TROSSLEY: Doesn't look like it.
              You look like you lost a brother.

DUGGAN: No, just a guy I met a few times
              At the Union Jack Club,
              Opposite the station.

TROSSLEY: You sure you're OK?
              You look like you seen a ghost.

DUGGAN: Fifteen years' service,
              But you never get used to it,
              The sudden death,
              The blood, the danger.
              I'll be all right.

TROSSLEY: You sure?

DUGGAN: I'm sure.

TROSSLEY: *[Doubtful]* If you say so…

DUGGAN: I'll be fine.
            It's awful, but it goes with the job.
            Right?

TROSSLEY: Right. *[Pause.]*
            I'll get us both some tea.

[Exits. Lights change to a single spot.]

DUGGAN: I denied Adam.
            I denied him three times.
            I am Judas and Peter both.
            I am so ashamed.

CROSSFADE TO THE INTERROGATION ROOM AGAIN

Scene Ten

[Lights change – interrogation room.

DUGGAN sits at the table. WILDER enters, carrying a briefcase. He opens the briefcase, extracts papers, and places them on the table in front of DUGGAN.]

WILDER: We found many things of interest
                When we cleared his lockers.

DUGGAN: We?

WILDER: The officers bagged up all his things.
                There were copies of *Gay News,*
                And a membership card –
                Campaign for Homosexual Equality

[FRASER enters, a ghost.]

FRASER: Everybody knew,
                All my mates knew.
                They would have covered for us,
                But they didn't have the locker key.
                That bastard RSM, he took my key.

DUGGAN: I told you,
                I warned you –

WILDER: What did you say? Who are you talking to?

129

FRASER: I always thought the RSM was gay,
The way he looked at me.

DUGGAN: Why did you keep things like those?

[He fingers the chain round his neck.]

FRASER: You kept my chain.

DUGGAN: This didn't need explaining.

WILDER: *[Seizing on the chain:]* What are you fingering that for?

DUGGAN: I'm nervous. You'd be nervous.

WILDER: *[Menacing]* Was it his? Did he give it to you?

DUGGAN: Who?

WILDER: Don't be simple. Fraser.
Did he give it to you?

DUGGAN: No!

FRASER: Say yes, say yes.

DUGGAN: It was a present from my mother.

WILDER: Really?

FRASER: What difference does it make?
             Nothing you can do will bring me back.

WILDER: When did your mother give it to you?
             [He consults his notes.] She died in nine-
                teen-sixty.
             You were thirteen.
             Not the obvious present for a young lad.

DUGGAN: She was religious. She hoped I'd be priest.

FRASER: Stop this.
             What's the point?
             Are you ashamed of me?

DUGGAN: No – I –

FRASER: Then stop being ashamed of yourself.

WILDER: We found a wedding ring on his hand,
             When we found his hand.
             Did you give that to him?

DUGGAN: No, his grandad –

FRASER: You can say it. *[A pause. DUGGAN
                struggles to tell the truth.]*

DUGGAN: He tried to give it to me,
             But I wouldn't have it.

I'm ashamed to say I turned him down.
And so he gave me this instead.

[WILDER attempts to grab the chain.]

WILDER: Give it here. *[They briefly struggle.]*

DUGGAN: I haven't taken it off all year.

WILDER: It's evidence.

DUGGAN: Fuck you.

WILDER: Don't make things worse.

DUGGAN: I'll give you a statement,
            What more do you want?

WILDER: You can have it back later.
            I'll give you that ring too,
            If you help us.

            You can make my job easier.

            I'm not a bad bloke.
            I've known a few of your sort,
            You're not bad blokes either.
            But we got to keep up morale,
            And you are bad for discipline.
            We can't have all the lads

Watching their arses
All the time.

FRASER: Say something. You must.
For my sake.
If you don't, I'll never speak to you again.
You don't deserve me,
And you won't deserve my memory.

[DUGGAN takes a deep breath.]

DUGGAN: Do you seriously think
I lusted for those beefy arses
In the barracks?
All those sweaty stinking bum holes
All those rough clumsy hands?
When I had the love – the *love* –
Of the most beautiful boy in the world?
Would Romeo go with any old slapper
When he had the love of Juliet?

FRASER: Whoa! I'm not the female to your male.

DUGGAN: Sorry, but I'm new to this.
I don't have the words.

FRASER: I will give you the words.
[Prompting] People think it's all about sex –

DUGGAN: People think it's all about sex –

FRASER: But it's more than that –

DUGGAN: It's more than that –

ADAM: It's quiet confidence and company,
            Sharing lives together –

DUGGAN: It's living with and for each other,
            It's being an item.

[FRASER slowly leaves. DUGGAN follows with his eyes.]

            Wanting to proclaim that we're an item.

[DUGGAN turns his attention to WILDER.]

DUGGAN: And yes, there's sex as well.
            The sex was fan-fucking-tastic.

WILDER: Careful, lad!

DUGGAN: I'm through with being careful.
            We had sex you can't imagine,
            And more of it than seemed possible.
            We fucked each other to exhaustion,
            And then we fucked again.
            And nothing you can say or do
            Can take away the memory
            Of one single moment of our happiness.

[Pause.]

WILDER: Are you prepared to sign a statement
                  To that effect?

DUGGAN: Why? Why should I make your job easy?

WILDER: It makes your life easier too.

DUGGAN: My life can never be easier.

WILDER: And what about the boy?
                  His reputation? His family?
                  If you confess, and say you led him on –

DUGGAN: That's not true –

WILDER: Which is more important?
                  Truth or reputation?
                  Truth or family feelings?

[A long pause. DUGGAN strips the insignia and the medal ribbon bar from his uniform. Hands it to WILDER.]

DUGGAN: What do you think?

WILDER: Thank you.

DUGGAN: But only in my own words.

WILDER: Agreed. You can write it in the cell.

[He gives DUGGAN some paper. Salutes him. DUGGAN refuses to salute back. WILDER smartly about-turns and exits. Lights fade. In the darkness, a priest intones a funeral oration offstage as music plays incorporating excerpts of the Last Post.]

PRIEST: Adam paid the ultimate price for serving his country, by giving his life. His sacrifice, and that of all the other soldiers who died, allows us to live the life we lead in freedom. It takes a special kind of person to face the possibility of war and death, especially a death that will save the lives of people you have never even met. John 15:13 says, 'Greater love has no one than this, than to lay down one's life for his friends.' Just as Jesus sacrificed his life so that we may be free, so too did Adam.

              'The Lord is near to those who have a broken heart,' says Psalm 34. Remembering our lost loved ones can be painful, especially if the grief is still fresh. But if you pour your hurt out to the Lord you can feel His comforting embrace upon you.

[The lights come up again.]

Scene Twelve

[FRASER is in an open coffin on a trestle. DUGGAN enters. He is now in civvies, a sober suit. He has a red and a white poppy in his buttonhole and is also wearing a pink triangle. He moves forward to look down at Adam's face. Very slowly he bends over and kisses him long and passionately. He stands up straight. Salutes him. Takes the triangle off his lapel and lays it in the coffin. Turns and marches to the edge of the stage. Lights fade on the coffin, leaving a single spot for DUGGAN.]

DUGGAN: That was nearly twenty years ago.
            Twenty years I had to fight –
            No pension, no medals, nothing left.

            I couldn't get a job.
            No school would have me,
            Not with my dishonourable discharge.
            I couldn't keep it quiet.
            And then there was Section Twenty-Eight.

            Four years it took to get a job
            As a nightshift cleaner.
            Lowest of the low.

            All those years they fobbed me off,
            The M.o.D.

            Excuses, evasions.
            Nothing changed.

Three hundred soldiers went in 1999,
Kicked out for the old, old story –
'Conduct prejudicial to good discipline'.

It took the European Court
Of Human Rights to bring
Sanity and compassion.

Regent's Park's forgotten now.
There's a plaque but otherwise
You'd never know.
Find it on the internet,
Hundreds of photos
Of the Hyde Park horses
And bloody Sefton,
But almost nothing of the bandstand.

Nasty bit of work, that Sefton.
Always biting jockeys.
He had a handler's fingers off –
That's why they called him Sharky.
Hopeless for a soldier's horse –
Kept trying to pass him off
On other regiments.
But still a hero, as he lived
Through sheer bloody-mindedness.
Unlike Adam.

[The general stage lights start slowly to grow.]

I don't regret being dismissed,
In spite of all the hurt.
It outed me, it took me to the place
I wanted, but could never dare to go.
Until then I could never show my sorrow.
I couldn't mourn
The partner I had lost –
My life partner for such a little while,
For such a shortened life.

A soldier faces to the front
To look life in the eyes,
Both friend and foe.
It will not do,
Always looking back
Over your shoulder,
Living in fear of discovery.
I hadn't any feelings,
I was only half a man
Until I was dismissed.

[The stage becomes fully lit.]

So thank you, Major Wilder,

[He turns toward the coffin.]

And thank you,
Oh my darling.
Adam, my love, thank you.

[DUGGAN produces a Pink Triangle wreath.]

Thank you, thank you.

[He lays the wreath as the lights fade.]

BLACKOUT

A Gay Century: 13

1984: Quarantine

A panic in 18 scenes

From an original idea by
Louise Parker Kelley

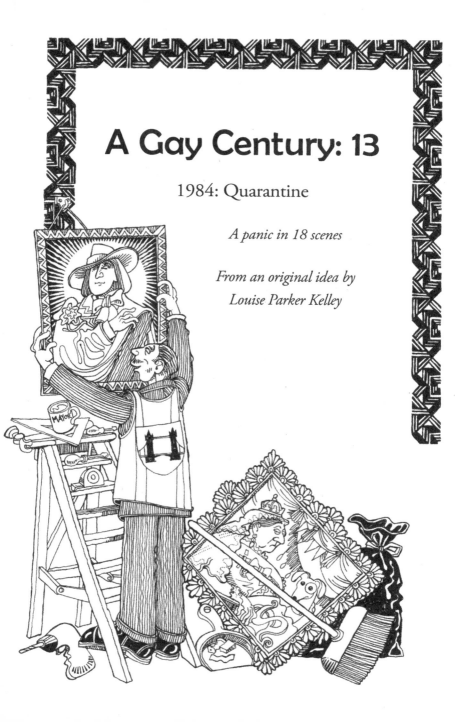

Above: *Newspaper headlines, 1984*
Below: *Norman Fowler and government campaign 1986*

Introduction

In October 1983, Consenting Adults in Public, at the time the only queer community theatre company in London, premiered the first play in the world about A.I.D.S., *AntiBody*, at the Cockpit Theatre. It was written mainly by Louise Parker Kelley, an American from Baltimore; I adapted it to make it fit a British situation – at that time the US was about two years ahead of Britain in its encounter with the epidemic, and Louise had written it out of her experience working in the Baltimore Community Centre and on the Gay and Lesbian Switchboard. I married Louise to allow her to stay in the country, so she could be part of the production. But that's another story.

A year later, Louise sent me a novel – I forget the title – about a not-so-futuristic situation where homosexuals were sent into quarantine on an isolated island where they were left to starve and die – genocide by attrition. While much of it was powerful, it suffered in my opinion from an over-simplistic and naïve belief in the power of the media to expose and remedy injustices. Even with Watergate, the *Washington Post* didn't end graft, corruption and the undermining of American democracy. Now *Fox News* is all-pervasive.

But I thought it merited something, and so I rewrote it as a 90-minute radio script and sent it to the BBC Drama department. They lost it. Two years later they found it, but told me that my pioneering work was now out of date. In the meantime there had been several other dramas about H.I.V./A.I.D.S., including episodes in soaps. Gay Sweatshop had presented *Compromised Immunity* in 1986, and other plays followed, including British productions of Larry Kramer's older *The Normal Heart* [Royal Court, 1986] and *As Is* [1987]. *As Is* itself seems somewhat indebted to *AntiBody*.

When it came to writing *The Gay Century*, it seemed obvious that the experience of the A.I.D.S./H.I.V. epidemic was probably the defining experience of homosexual life for anyone born between 1920 and 1970 – and not just for men; lesbians in remarkable solidarity stepped up to the plate to help and campaign about a virus which barely affected them at all. Because of this centrality to the century, I decided that this play too would be full length. It stands at over two hours, with an interval. Only *A Shot at the Future*, about parenting, is as long.

I thought back to Louise's work, unpublished and neglected by the BBC. Much of what it predicted had never come to pass, but this really didn't matter, because the play was a remarkably accurate depiction of what it felt like within the gay community in 1984–85, when dystopia seemed not only imminent, but already upon us. As the prologue says,

This is not the way it was,
It is the way we felt it was.
This is not what happened,
This is what we felt might happen.
And it did.
In our nightmares.

It is almost impossible to convey the extent to which this hung over our lives, seeped into our nightmares and permeated our sense of identity and worth. This is the time when the disease was called GRID [Gay Related Immune Deficiency]; when papers were full of accounts of the 'gay plague', or 'gay pneumonia'; when there were serious calls in Parliament to isolate homosexuals on islands; when women were sacked because their *husbands* had contracted the virus. There was no treatment, no protective vaccine and no cure. It was an almost certain death sentence, with the average length of time from diagnosis to death being ten months. Even action which was intended as positive, such as the Government's admonitory campaign to encourage safer sex, was accompanied by images out of horror films – icebergs and tombstones and graveyards. All the events in this libretto, however outlandish, are suggested by real incidents.

I replaced Louise's optimistic resolution of the black impasse with something I thought altogether more plausible, which was to have an influential member of the government find that someone close to them had contracted H.I.V./A.I.D.S. There is nothing like personal experience to change hearts and minds, or mobilise action; or so I thought. One hoped that the same thing would happen with Covid-19 and a Prime Minister who only weeks previously was still boasting that he was shaking hands with everybody, before having a near-death experience. However, there is no sign of Boris Johnson being chastened, while exposure to the virus only convinced Donald Trump that he was the Messiah.

All characters in this are fictional, with the one exception of Norman Fowler, now Lord Fowler of Sutton Coldfield. He was Secretary of State for Health and Social Services 1981–87. It is a kind of tribute to him, in that from everything one hears, he underwent a remarkable conversion from the kind of knee-jerk homophobic reactions which characterised other ministers[5], to embracing the idea of working with organisations of LGBT people, learning from them, and championing the cause of LGBT rights as a means of helping to contain and control the virus. Fowler went on to remain involved in the cause of fighting H.I.V./A.I.D.S. long after his stint in the DHSS was over. He joined the boards of several H.I.V./A.I.D.S. charities in the 1990s, advocated for an EU ambassador with responsibility for A.I.D.S., in the 2000s, campaigned for equal marriage, and in 2014 published a kind of sequel to the government's 'Don't Die Of Ignorance' campaign which he had masterminded. This was *AIDS: Don't Die of Prejudice*.

I sent Lord Fowler a copy of the libretto of *Quarantine*, explaining what I had done, and he was happy to have his name used in this way, despite the depiction of his [fictional] family. Suffice it to say that he does not have a son called Sebastian.

Because this story has a panoramic focus, with many characters, it is written with a flexible open stage, minimal costume changes, and quick switches between multiple characters for each singer. In the event of finding a produc-

---

[5] He is reputed to have had to ask a civil servant to explain what a blow-job was. He was appalled when he was told. This rumour is retained in the script.

tion with a company with more resources, the roles can be spread between more singers.

This play is one – *Skin Deep* is another – where reference to popular songs of the day is made. I find it impossible to conceive a libretto about gay life from the 1920s onward where pop songs don't play some part in the experience and the psyche of lesbians and gay men, and that entanglement becomes closer and more urgent, the closer we come to the twenty-first century and the ubiquitous dance scene.

It has to be here, very specifically, in the scenes with the 'Bar Flies', the apolitical lesbians and gay men whose most earnest desire is to have a quiet drink in a cosy pub they can call Home. They play and dance the moves of *YMCA*, which was a popular dance favourite from its appearance in 1978 and throughout the early 80s, something which binds them into a community, and also becomes a symbolic act of defiance.

But I must repeat, this isn't a history lesson but a fantasy set in the then-future [it goes up to the mid-90s]. It was all too plausible to our beleaguered selves in 1984.

CAST

Four singers play multiple roles; these are not necessarily as I have allocated them at this stage, but they must work so that singers have time to transition to the next role.

MEZZO-SOPRANO:
Vita, Ruth, Judge, Ellie, Kitty, Barfly 1, Nicola, Anna

COUNTER-TENOR:
Sebastian, Burgess, Ryan, David, Richard, Barfly 2

TENOR:
Ian, Stuart, Max, Inspector, Barfly 3, Nick, Shaun

BARITONE:
Interrogation voice, Fowler, Clive, Bar Raider, Gary Northgate, Andrew, Scientist

SETTINGS

Multiple settings, light furniture – a chair as needed. For The Island, a bunk bed, which can be covered up for other scenes.

INSTRUMENTS

Piano, baritone/tenor sax [doubled] and alto sax.

QUARANTINE

ACT ONE

Prologue

[All Four Actors face the audience in a row.]

QUARTET: This is not the way it was,
It is the way we felt it was.
This is not what happened,
This is what we felt might happen.
And it did,
In our nightmares.

BLACKOUT

Scene One

[A harsh siren. A searchlight. A running figure, caught in the searchlight, freezes.]

VOICE: Name, age, address,
Names of all sexual contacts
In the last five years.
Their addresses too.
Did any have any symptoms?

IAN: I'm not sick.

VOICE: Name, age, address,
Names of all sexual contacts
In the last five years,
Their addresses and their symptoms.

IAN: You know my name and address –
Ian Lucas.
I filled out the forms
In triplicate.
How am I meant to remember
Everyone I've known?
Every pick-up at a party,
Every chat-up in a bar?
This was the seventies, remember,
'Sex and drugs and rock and roll
Is all my brain and body needs'.

VOICE:	Please try and remember.
IAN:	I told you, I'm not sick.
VOICE:	Your test was positive.
IAN:	Impossible! What is this? I came to get a check-up Like everyone must, I filled out all the forms, You take the blood, You make me wait. And now some voice is talking to me, Asking the impossible. Come and talk face to face.
VOICE:	*[Patient:]* The liquid turned red – Positive. You have HTLV-3, And now you must be kept apart From others who are healthy, To protect the general public From the Plague.
IAN:	I'm not going *there*.
VOICE:	You must obey the law. All those in contact with the virus Must agree to seek treatment

At the treatment centre
On the Isle of Man.

IAN: Queer Island! I'm not going. *[Pause.]*
I can't have it. *[Pause.]*
I'm not gay.

BLACKOUT

Scene Two

[An illegal gay bar run in someone's private house. Gay disco music – Village People – quietly in the background. Three shallow Bar Flies stare glumly into their drinks.]

BARFLY 1:   I used to love to dance to this.

BARFLY 2:   So did I. Remember at Heaven?

BARFLY 3:   There'd be hundreds on the floor…

ALL: Those were the days.

[The disco music has faded.]

BARFLY 1:   It was the biggest disco in Europe.

BARFLY 2:   I went to the leather bar.

BARFLY 3:   I went to the backroom.

ALL: Those were the days.

BARFLY 3:   And now there's nowhere…

BARFLY 2:   All closed down…

BARFLY 1:   For women and for men.
              It's not as if the lesbians are at risk –

Lesbians don't get it.

ALL: Or so they say.
Who knows?

BARFLY 3:   Who knows anything anymore?
There's nothing on the news.

BARFLY 2:   If they still had lesbian bars,
Perhaps they'd let the gay boys in.

BARFLY 3:   Perhaps they'd sneak in, in drag.

BARFLY 1:   I'll drink to that. To you, fellas.
[She grimaces.] This gin is piss.

BARFLY 2:   Of course, it's watered…

BARFLY 3:   At these prices? That's outrageous!
It's ten times what it used to be
When gay bars were still legal.

ALL: Those were the days.

BARFLY 1:   There aren't even measures any more,
Barry slops it in, as little as he feels like.

BARFLY 2:   Sometimes it barely covers
The bottom of the glass.

BARFLY 3:   You can't blame Barry
              For wanting to make money while he can,
              The risks he runs.

BARFLY 1:   It's not so risky;
              A basement in a private house…
              Nobody will notice.
              We're very quiet,
              And looking at you,
              No-one would suspect
              That you were queer.

BARFLY 3:   Anyone could tell on us –
              A nosey neighbour,
              Smelling a rat –

BARFLY 2:   A little queer rat – Eeek, doll! Eeek!

[They laugh, then there is a sudden melancholy silence.]

BARFLY 2:   Remember when there were real measures –
              Optics – you always got the same amount,
              By law.

ALL: Those were the days.

ALL: You could see –

BARFLY 1:   A girl –

BARFLIES 2 & 3:   A guy —

ALL: across the room.
                    You could ask them for a dance,
                    You could buy them a drink,
                    You could spin them a line.

BARFLY 1:   What's a nice girl like you
                    Doing in a place like this?

BARFLY 2:   Do you come here often?

BARFLY 3:   Has anyone ever told you
                    You have beautiful eyes?

ALL: Those were the days:
                    All gone now, all shut down.

[There is a siren in the distance.]

BARFLY 1:   Is that coming this way?

BARFLY 2:   I can't tell.

BARFLY 3:   I think it's going into the Square.

[It gets louder.]

BARFLY 1:   It's getting closer.

BARFLY 3:   It won't be coming here,
No-one knows about us.

BARFLY 2:   We've been very discreet –

BARFLY 3:   The door is locked,
The blinds are drawn –

BARFLY 2:   There's nothing to show from outside.

[The siren is now very loud indeed.]

BARFLY 1:   *[Calling:]* Hey, Barry! We've got to get
out of here!

BARFLY 2:   There's a little window in the toilet,
We could go over the garden wall.

BARFLY 3:   You'd never get your fat arse through the
window.

BARFLY 2:   Bitch!

BARFLY 1:   Barry, let us out of here,
It's a raid! Where is the man?
[To the others:] Pretend it's just a private
party.
I'll be your wife, if anyone asks.

BARFLY 2:   Yes, dear.

BARFLY 3:   Homosexual, moi?

[The door bursts open and a policeman in full biological suit, wearing rubber gloves, with a machine gun, stands in the doorway. The scene freezes.]

BLACKOUT

Scene Three

[Spotlight again. RUTH, a tired young woman, is caught in it. She is dressed in a dress which is designed to allure, but has seen better days.]

RUTH: God give me strength!
There's not much longer…

VOICE: I have to ask you again:
Names of your sexual contacts!

RUTH: Fuck you! I'm a whore!
You think I ask their names?
You think they tell me?

VOICE: You're going to intensive care
In the Isle of Man.

RUTH: Man! Ha!
It was men who got me here,
Could have been any of them.

VOICE: Names –

RUTH: In any case, I don't care.
I'll die before I get there.

VOICE: Your condition is not far advanced.

RUTH: What do you know?
D'you know how long I've lived with this?
D'you know how long I've kept this hidden?
Passing out in toilets,
Throat like sandpaper.
People cross the street
Cos they know you've got it,
They won't breathe the same air.
Weight falling off so fast
Like you're ice cream melting in the sun.
And you just say 'I'm on a diet'...
Well, now I'm dying
And you can't stop me!

VOICE: Sexual contacts in the last ten years...?

RUTH: I'll cheat you yet.

BLACKOUT

Scene Four

[A BBC Studio. VITA van DYKE is a TV Anchor. FOWLER and SEBASTIAN enter; FOWLER is Minister of Health, SEBASTIAN his P.A. SEBASTIAN ushers him to a seat.]

SEB: Minister…

FOWLER: How do I look?

SEB: *[Surveys him critically, brushes his sleeve.]*
                Fine, minister.
                Authoritative. *[To unseen crew:]* We're
                    ready now.

[Lights become brighter for transmission.]

VITA: For ten years now
                The virus
                Has been spreading at a frightening rate.
                It's been called the gay plague,
                Gay Related Immune Deficiency,
                GRID.
                Though others do get it,
                Homosexual men predominate.
                Now that the cases number
                In the tens of thousands,
                Hospitals, doctors,
                Hospices, clinics,
                Have been unable to cope,

Despite the use of private medical suppliers
And the new compulsory insurance.
For five years now
The government has experimented
With internment of the infected,
To combat the epidemic.
I have with me
The Minister of Health
And Disease Prevention,
Sir Norman Fowler.

FOWLER: I must take issue with you.
               This is not internment.
               The Man Community
               Has the full support
               Of many of the caring charities
               Working with the victims.
               It was an altruistic enterprise,
               And homosexuals could see that.
               They would have set it up
               If we had not.

VITA: But not all have co-operated,
               And not all victims are gay.

FOWLER: But homosexuals form the majority.

VITA: Still, many people resist a screening,
               And many hide that they are gay
               In case they're sent to Man.

FOWLER: This is a public health issue.
               There will always be selfish people
               Who think they are above the law.
               But fears are groundless;
               Only the sick are sent,
               No need to send the healthy.

VITA: But what about the healthy
               Who tend the sick?
               The healthy gays with medical skills?
               We have reports that they are sent.

FOWLER: There are some volunteers
               Who want to help
               In this humanitarian crisis.
               We welcome every effort,
               We don't enquire their sexual orientation.
               Clergy, counsellors and nurses
               All are needed urgently.

VITA: They don't have any choice.

FOWLER: That's not true.

VITA: How can we know that?
               The media aren't allowed to see for them-
                    selves.

FOWLER: Surely you can see, Vita,
               That we must preserve the privacy

Of the infected victims?
We're very strict about data protection –
And rightly so.

VITA: So what is life like there?

FOWLER: I haven't actually visited, of course.
The virus is infectious, after all.
But I can assure you –
And the British public –
Victims have the finest care available,
And everybody else is being protected.
Thank you.

[The lights become slightly less intense. FOWLER and SEBASTIAN move to the edge of the stage.]

FOWLER: *[To SEBASTIAN:]* How was I?

SEB: Excellent. In control as usual. *[He exits.]*

VITA: *[Still at the presenter's desk, over those two lines:]*
That was the Minister for Health
And Disease Prevention.
And finally, some late news.
The death has been announced
Of the Earl of Eden,
Till recently a junior minister
At the Department of Health,

And government spokesman on health
In the House of Lords.

FOWLER: Good God. Boofie?

VITA: The Earl, who was fifty-three,
Had been suffering from pneumonia
And died of complications.

FOWLER: I was working with him
Only two weeks ago.
I was at school with him!
He was my fag in his first year;
He warmed my slippers,
He made my toast.

VITA: He was probably best known
For appearing on Tango Fandango
Two years ago, when his cheerful
Energy combined with two left feet
Endeared him to viewers everywhere.
The weather will be mild and cloudy,
Clearing for a cold but sunny morning.
That is the end of the news.
Good night.

FOWLER: *[Over VITA:]*
Always thought it was a shame
He never married.
[A look of horror on his face, as a penny drops.]

You don't think – ?
He couldn't possibly be –
He didn't look as if he was –
He looked perfectly normal,
Just like anyone else.
Well I'll be –
I would never have guessed.

[SEBASTIAN reappears.]

SEBASTIAN: Julian Sharpe from Sky News
Would like a word with you
About the death of the Earl of Eden.

FOWLER: I just heard. So sad.

SEBASTIAN: The news said fifty-three.

FOWLER: Three years younger than me.
What a waste!
Wheel young Julian in.
Damn fine chap. Hard worker.
Loyal friend. Great company.
Poor old Boofie…
We had some great times…

BLACKOUT

Scene Five

[The spotlight. ELLIE. She has Kaposi's Sarcoma lesions on her face.]

VOICE: How long have you concealed this?

ELLIE: I don't know. Three months, perhaps.
               Can I have some dope now?

VOICE: We do not supply intravenous drugs.

ELLIE: They promised me, if I came in
               And told about the others that I knew,
               I could shoot up for free.

VOICE: They told you wrong.

ELLIE: I gave you all the names of my friends,
               Addresses where I had them,
               For those not on the streets.

VOICE: What about your sexual partners?

ELLIE: You think I have sex with a face like this?

VOICE: You needed money for drugs.

ELLIE: No.

VOICE: Any money. From anyone.
            There's people just don't care.

ELLIE: No

VOICE: We'll make you take a lie detector test.

ELLIE: Do it. What the fuck do I care?
            Just let me have a hit.
            I hurt so much.

VOICE: The receptionist will find someone to
               take you.
            Officially we don't supply methadone –

ELLIE: But it's a well-known secret...

VOICE: And afterwards you will come back
            [Pause.]
            You will come back to tell us more.

                        BLACKOUT

Scene Six

[The office of the Campaign for Gay Equality [CGE]. A filing cabinet. ANNA and NICK.]

ANNA: I've had a subpoena
           To appear at the Old Bailey.
           It's a kind of test case
           About data protection.
           I've been ordered to hand over
           The records of all members
           And addresses of supporters,
           Plus all the correspondence
           Which the Campaign for Gay Equality
           Has on file; letters from other gay groups
           Around the country and from abroad,
           Letters asking for advice
           From frightened teenagers:
           People are going to be arrested
           For wanting legal advice.
           The police came,
           Demanded I hand them over.
           I asked to see a search warrant,
           They scratched their heads and went away.
           No-one asks to see a warrant these days.
           They came back later with their warrant.
           By then I'd got a lot of information
           Away from the office.

NICK: Really? Where?

ANNA: You can't expect me to tell you that.

NICK: But I'm the Campaign Legal Officer.

ANNA: And that's precisely why my lips are sealed.
            You're fatally respectful of the law –
            They'd whistle and you'd have to run.
            So now they're hauling me to court...

NICK: If you don't trust me, how can I help?

ANNA: I need advice.
            I don't want anyone with me,
            In case they trump up charges of abetting,
            Or maybe a conspiracy.
            I'll defend myself okay,
            But the law has got me all confused.
            We're meant to have our privacy protected,
            We've had data protection
            These several years,
            And yet this recent CDA...

NICK: Communicable Diseases Act, yes

ANNA: ... makes it an offence
            To withhold information
            Which might help prevent
            The spread of disease.
            Which one will the court uphold?

NICK: You can always argue your address lists
               Will not help the fight against infection.
               Whether that will wash I can't predict.
               Judges these days are as panicked
               As everybody else.
               The government could argue
               It needs to know
               The people most at risk,
               The people to be tested,
               The people that they need to check
               Whether they *have* been tested;
               A question of management,
               A question of priorities.

[A siren in the distance.]

               'Of course we'd love to recognise
               Your civil liberties,
               But this is an emergency:
               A national emergency.'

ANNA: Nick, sometimes you're terrifying…
               No chance then?

NICK: Not a snowball's chance in hell.
               Not with the *Daily Mail* on their backs,
               Demanding that we're all locked up.

ANNA: 'For our own protection…'

[The siren getting closer.]

NICK: You hear that?

ANNA: Perhaps it's someone else –

NICK: Perhaps it's not.

ANNA: I'm going to court next week, that can't
            be for us.

NICK: Perhaps they prefer not to wait,
            Perhaps they don't want the publicity,
            Perhaps it's 'out of sight, so out of mind.'

*[A policeman in a biological suit appears in the doorway, the
one who raided the bar in Scene Two. They can't help giggling
at the sight – they have not seen this before.]*

POLICEMAN: Anna Duncan? Anna Matilda Duncan?

NICK: Matilda?

ANNA: Shut up.

POLICEMAN: This is serious.

ANNA: You look ridiculous,
            Out of some crappy sci-fi B-movie.

POLICEMAN: Anna Matilda Duncan,
               You are under arrest
               For concealing the whereabouts
               Of infected persons.

ANNA: I don't know any infected persons.

POLICEMAN: Oh really?

ANNA: None that haven't been rounded up for
               treatment.

POLICEMAN: Darling, how many members do you
               have?

ANNA: About ten thousand –
               And don't you 'darling' me.

POLICEMAN: And do you seriously think, darling,
               Not one in ten thousand has been
                  infected?
               Not one?
               And we'll find him – or her – or
                  them,
               Now testing is compulsory.

[He starts looking through the filing cabinet.]

ANNA: *[A touch of triumph:]* It's useless looking
               there,

The thing is empty.

NICK: I am Ms Duncan's solicitor
                  And a UN Human Rights observer.
                  Where are you taking her?

POLICEMAN: Your name? Your ID card?
                  Have you been tested?

NICK: Nick Sherringham and yes I have.
                  Where are you taking her?

POLICEMAN: I think I'd better take you in as well.

NICK: For what?

POLICEMAN: Conspiracy to obstruct the preven-
                      tion of disease –
                  A very serious crime
                  Under the Contagious Diseases Act.

                  BLACKOUT

Scene Seven

[The TV studio again. SEBASTIAN and MINISTER. No presenter.]

SEB: I have your notes here.

MINISTER: I won't need notes.
                I'll keep it simple and direct,
                Look them in the eye.
                You stand by the director
                And tell them when to cut.

SEB: Yes, minister.

[Lights bright for broadcasting.]

FOWLER: Good evening.
                My name is Norman Fowler,
                Broadcasting on the
                National TV Channel
                On behalf of the Government.
                There has been a great deal of nonsense
                Talked about safe sex.
                People seem to think
                They can protect themselves.
                'Have fewer partners,
                Have healthy partners,
                Don't sleep with Americans,'
                That's what they say:

The permissive voices,
The irresponsible voices.
Let us be quite clear,
There is no such thing as safe sex,
Except within the stable loving bond
Of Marriage. Man and woman.
The government believes in
Victorian values,
Procreation of children,
Responsibility,
Self-control.
Just say no,
It's as simple as that;
Whether you're a teenage girl
Who might get pregnant,
Or a young boy
Approached by an older man
And offered glamour and excitement.
Oscar Wilde said,
'I can resist everything except tempta-
    tion',
And we all know what happened
To Oscar Wilde.
Let that be an awful warning to you.
Just say no.

[Lights change.]

How was that, Sebastian?

SEB: Very strong, minister.
                You left the viewer in no doubt at all.

FOWLER: Are you all right, Sebastian?
                You look a little tired,
                You've been overworking.
                Get away for the weekend –
                Brighton or somewhere.
                Fresh air'd do you good.

SEB: I was thinking of Amsterdam.

FOWLER: See the Rembrandts? Excellent.

[They exit.]

FADE TO BLACKOUT

Scene Eight

[The single spotlight. RYAN, a boy of about seven, in it.]

RYAN: I want to go to Queer Island.

VOICE: It's not called Queer Island,
               It's the Man Health Facility.

RYAN: Everyone calls it Queer Island.

VOICE: Why do you want to go there?

RYAN: Cos I'm queer.

VOICE: No you're not.

RYAN: How do you know?

VOICE: If you were homosexual, we would know.

RYAN: They think I'm queer at school.
               When they have swimming lessons
               They won't let me in the pool,
               In case they catch the plague from me.
               When I started at the new school,
               Parents kept their kids away.

VOICE: You were tested. You don't have the
                   disease.

RYAN: My mum has it, she took drugs.

VOICE: And now she's being treated.

RYAN: I miss my Mum –
               I want to go to Queer Island.

VOICE: We don't want you to be at risk.
               You could catch something there.
               We don't think she can cope with you.
               She allowed herself to be infected,
               She can't be a good mother.
               There's thousands of gay men there;
               You could be exposed to – brutalisation.
               You have a nice new Christian foster
                    mum.

RYAN: I want my real mum.

BLACKOUT

Scene Nine

[The Isle of Man camp. CLIVE and DAVID being shown round by KITTY, an old hand. CLIVE has a suitcase. A bunk bed.]

KITTY: These will be yours –
            And that's your lockers.

CLIVE: Top or bottom?

DAVID: I'll toss you for it.

CLIVE: Any excuse…

DAVID: I don't need an excuse. *[Moves closer sexily.]*

KITTY: I wouldn't if I were you. *[Points –]*
            Hidden cameras. They're everywhere.
            Inmates get split up
            If they start to get fresh,
            Just in case…

CLIVE: Inmates, are we?

KITTY: What would you prefer?
            Patients?
            There are no medicines –
            A disease without a cure,
            And half the 'inmates' don't have it anyway.

Do you have it?
I ask because this ward
Is for the well,
For those who wouldn't take
The government directives;
Who fought and protested,
Or sheltered someone with the virus.

DAVID: That's me.

CLIVE: He sheltered me.

KITTY: Excuse me? You must be in the wrong
place.

CLIVE: Except I wasn't. The test was wrong;
It was a false positive.

DAVID: The doctors wouldn't believe it,
They thought he had disguised it.

CLIVE: After three months I was still in the clear.

DAVID: But I was still guilty of hiding an infected
person.
Even though he wasn't,
I hid him cos I thought he was.

CLIVE: Already they had given me
The tattoo that proved it.

[He rolls up his sleeve and shows a number tattooed on his arm.]

I'll never wear short sleeves again.

KITTY: That's totally crazy.

CLIVE: So what are we, now we're not patients?
Prisoners?

KITTY: *[Ironic]* You can leave at any time.
Except there is no boat off the island,
And if you try to swim away,
Patrols will fire warning shots
That happen to be fatal.

DAVID: I'll take the top.

CLIVE: Of course you'll take the top;
Why change the habit of a lifetime?

KITTY: You know what I really miss
On the Island?

DAVID: What do you miss?

KITTY: No pets:
No dogs, no cats, no parakeets,
Not even a fucking goldfish.
You didn't have pets, did you?

CLIVE: No – David has allergies.

DAVID: Blame it on me!

KITTY: Well if you did have pets, you don't have
                   now.
                They all get put down
                In case they're infected.
                Don't even bother to test them,
                They're only animals.
                We had a Labrador bitch, Trudy... *[She
                   trails off sadly.]*
                [Outburst:] To think I volunteered!
                A health colony! And I believed it!
                I had a partner, Stephen,
                He's a haemophiliac
                And he was diagnosed,
                Poisoned by government-issue blood.
                I had a test, negative, but
                We couldn't bear to be apart,
                So I came with him.
                I thought, 'It's not for long.
                He'll die, for sure,
                But with me by his bed.
                I've tested negative,
                So when it's over
                I can leave when I want to.'
                How stupid can you get?
                'Perhaps you've been infected here;
                You need another six months' quarantine'.

And then another.
Then another.

CLIVE: I'm sorry – what's your name?

KITTY: Kitty.

CLIVE: Clive. My partner David.

KITTY: The bathroom is at the far end,
            The toilet is next to it.
            One shower and two toilets
            For twenty-four inmates,
            Three with severe incontinence.

CLIVE: Isn't there a hospital?

KITTY: What for? A hospice, not a hospital.
            I'm sorry I'm not cheering you up.
            We had another suicide this morning.

DAVID: Was it a relief? A blessing in disguise?

CLIVE: Since there's no cure…

KITTY: There were no symptoms!
            No infection, no swollen glands,
            No Kaposi's. Not even a sore throat
            Or a yeast infection.

DAVID: Perhaps he was taking back control.

KITTY: She. She not he. She.

CLIVE: Suicide demonstrates free will.

KITTY: She was just depressed;
            She was sure she'd die of it one day…

DAVID: We'll all die one day…

CLIVE: You're all heart.

KITTY: You'll learn.
            It's very depressing to be with
            Ill people all the time.

DAVID: When do we get the rest of our things?

KITTY: What things?

CLIVE: We had to leave our trunk at reception.

KITTY: Forget it.
            It's been nicked by now,
            Or ransacked.
            Shoes are pretty popular round here,
            But everything can be sold or swapped.
            Did you have any jeans?
            Or toothpaste or shampoo

Or pills or books?
If you did, you don't have any more.
Stuff's in short supply in Man –
Clothes and hope –
It's why we have to guard the crematorium,
So no-one robs the dead.
You should try to barter for a lock
For that locker,
Or soon you won't have even what you've
    got.

DAVID: I'm starting to get hungry.

KITTY: Supper is at five,
Lights out at nine.
They've cut the rations yet again –
500 grams of bread,
50 grams of fat,
200 grams of soya.

DAVID: That's absurd. They've got to feed us.

KITTY: Why? What use are we to them?
Listen, they don't *have* to do anything.
Some clever boffin
Worked out scientifically
How many calories we need
And how much protein.
They make it as cheaply as they can,
And most of the vegetables are rotten.

Of course you get more if you work.
The best gig is the crematorium,
Laying out the bodies,
Taking out the teeth,
The eyes and so on,
For medical research.

CLIVE: And making sure that no-one else
            Gets to pillage corpses.

KITTY: Exactly. Well, you know we all
            Want more research.

DAVID: I won't do it. I refuse to work.

KITTY: Then you will starve
            And by degrees, you'll die.
            Like so many have before you,
            And so many more will soon.
            Welcome to the death camp!

BLACKOUT – INTERVAL

ACT TWO

Scene Ten

[RICHARD is in a wheelchair; NICOLA pushes him. She is wearing a mask and rubber gloves.]

RICHARD: I want to go to the treatment centre.

NICOLA: Calm down. We're arranging it for you.

RICHARD: But how long will it take?
I can't stand this hospital any more:
Everyone in masks and gloves
Whenever they come near me.

NICOLA: You are infectious,
It's simple Health and Safety.

RICHARD: But I'm a human being.
Everyone behaves as if I didn't count –
I have feelings too.
This loneliness is killing me.
Even the porters won't come near me;
They leave my meals outside the door,
Then knock and run away.

NICOLA: They're afraid; you can't blame them.

RICHARD: This is a hospital, they should know better.

The cleaning staff will only clean my room
In biological suits and masks –
They're made with asbestos, for fuck's sake.
How safe is that?

NICOLA: No need for language.

RICHARD: They're for nuclear fallout, not a virus.

NICOLA: They use them when there's a plague.

RICHARD: Oh yes, I was forgetting.
This is the gay plague.
I thought when I came in
There'd be some respite
From all the headlines:
'Gay plague threatens babies' –
'My son's gay plague agony' –
'Gay plague spreads – innocent victims'.
But of course, I'm one of the guilty ones,
I'm gay, and I deserve to die.
And thanks to my tattoo…

[He indicates his forearm.]

…Everyone can know.

NICOLA: Of course you don't deserve to die. No-
            one does.

RICHARD: Tell that to the lads
            Who daubed the words on my front door,
            PLAGUE and POUF,
            In blood-red letters two feet high.
            Tell that to the mob
            That came and smashed my windows.
            They would have done me over,
            Till I pointed out they'd spill my blood,
            And then I'd give it to them.
            They couldn't cope with that.

NICOLA: Stop dwelling on the past.
            You'll have a new life soon
            In the Isle of Man.

RICHARD: They call it isolation, but
            I couldn't feel more isolated
            Than I am now,
            And I'll be with my own kind.

NICOLA: You will. As soon as your papers come
              through.

RICHARD: I will be able to take my dog, won't I?

NICOLA: Of course you will.

BLACKOUT

Scene Eleven

[A court. JUDGE, STUART the defendant, Mr BURGESS for the Defence. STUART is wearing a lovely flowery dress, a picture hat and matching shoes.]

JUDGE: Let me be clear:
The defendant broke the law.
That is the only issue in this trial,
The reasons do not matter.

[He finally notices what STUART is wearing. Goggles a bit.]

JUDGE: *[Incredulous]* Do you always dress like this?

STUART: Not always, your majesty. *[A deep curtsey.]*

JUDGE: You will address me as Your Honour.
Why are you dressed like this?

STUART: I like to look nice when I go out.

JUDGE: Well, remove the hat at least.

STUART: No, I couldn't possibly do that.

JUDGE: I say remove it.

STUART: No, never. I'd rather die.

JUDGE: Why on earth not?

STUART: It goes with the shoes.
            Do you want to ruin the ensemble?

JUDGE: Are you showing contempt of court?

STUART: *[Mimicking Mae West:]* No, your honour,
            I'm doin' my best to hide it.
            [To BURGESS:] He's the perfect straight
                man.

JUDGE: Order in court!

BURGESS: *[To STUART:]* Behave yourself.
            [To JUDGE:] Your honour,
            The defendant does not deny the charge
            He trespassed on government property
            To sabotage computers.
            He admits criminal damage,
            But he pleads justification
            Or mitigation.

STUART: I want to tell you why.

BURGESS: The case is being heard in camera
            Under the Contagious Diseases Act 1990.
            There are no reporters.

JUDGE: In that case I have no objection

If he wants to tell us how he broke the law.

STUART: A jury would understand.

JUDGE: Under the CDA there are no juries.
               Proceed.

BURGESS: Tell the judge what happened on June
               28th, 1994.

STUART: We were tired of waiting for justice.
               It was the twenty-fifth anniversary
               Of the Stonewall Riots –
               Not that you'd know it from the papers.
               When we read of the new database,
               All the police records,
               All those who had ever
               Been to clubs,
               To gay demonstrations,
               To clap clinics,
               On mailing lists,
               We had to do something.
               But nobody cared.
               We wanted to fight back,
               And I was chosen.
               We knew where it was held, the database:
               In Newcastle, at the Ministry of Health
               And Disease Prevention.
               All we needed was the codes
               To get into the building,

And to the computer room.
And a sympathetic night guard.
I dressed as a painter,
With caustic soda in a paint pot,
The rest you know.
They couldn't arrest me
Before I had destroyed
At least half the files they had.
Maybe they have copies somewhere else,
But it was a symbolic protest,
Against the systematic persecution
Of lesbians and gays,
And of PWAs.

JUDGE: The access to the codes was top secret,
            Restricted to most senior personnel.
            You still refuse to name your accomplices?

STUART: I do. You can torture me if you like –

JUDGE: Mr Feather, the British state
            Does not torture people.

STUART: Ha!

BURGESS: The defence was not suggesting that it did.

STUART: You only abuse the sick.

JUDGE: In view of the testimony of the defendant

I find him guilty.
He is sentenced to preventive detention
On the Isle of Man indefinitely.

BURGESS: My lord, there is no evidence of infection.

JUDGE: And your point is?
He is clearly a threat to the security of the
State.

STUART: Fascism is more contagious than any
disease.
[To BURGESS:] At least we've got the
story on the record.

JUDGE: The defendant's testimony will be stricken
From the record. Take him down.

BLACKOUT

Scene Twelve

[The sound of a football crowd. GARY NORTHGATE giving his team a last minute pep-talk before they go on the field. SHAUN, one of the players, appears onstage as soon as he can, in kit, and with the ball.]

GARY: Lads, it won't be easy,
I'll be the first to admit.
City are the tops
And we're way down the league.
The bookies say it's five-to-one against us
To take the cup.
But the crowd is on our side,
Let's give them a good show.
You've watched the City games,
You know their weaknesses.
Billy, you must stick to Hahn like glue.
Their backs are weak, so split them up.
Go straight in, all out, from the start.
I know that you can do it,
And you must know it too.
Just one other thing:
We've had this note from the FA
I've got to pass to you.
It's about A.I.D.S., as they call it now,
And what we've got to do;
Or rather, what we should refrain from
    doing.

You must stop hugging when you score a
    goal.
Of course, no kissing either.
I know you've got to celebrate
And let off steam,
But punch the air alone –
That's an order.

If we win – of course we'll win –
There'll be no drinking bubbly
From the cup. No sharing glasses,
No more sharing baths.

SHAUN: Aw, skipper. We all look forward to that.
                Relaxing in the steam,
                A bit of larking around.

GARY: We cannot be too careful
                At a time like this.

                Separate showers only.
                And don't swap shirts with the other team
                After the game.

SHAUN: That's not fair. I was collecting them.

GARY: The coaches will have mouthpieces
                To give the kiss of life,
                And rubber gloves
                For treating any wounds.

After, they'll destroy
All buckets and all sponges.

SHAUN: The game will never be the same again.
Why are we doing all this, boss?

GARY: The FA has a duty to protect you.

SHAUN: I don't see the point.
Everybody knows
Footballers aren't queer.

BLACKOUT

Scene Thirteen

[The sound of waves on a shore. KITTY, CLIVE sitting on the edge of a cliff.]

KITTY: There's planes fly over all the time,
           One of them must see us,
           If we can get a fire going.

CLIVE: I hope this works.

KITTY: I don't see why it shouldn't,
           If David can get hold of ethanol.

CLIVE: Clever of him to volunteer
           For the medical supplies.

KITTY: Medical supplies! It's just to sterilise
           The gear the staff use,
           And their little accomplices,
           So they don't catch anything.

CLIVE: I wonder if he'll get enough.

[Enter DAVID with a large flagon, the size of one you'd mount on an office water cooler.]

DAVID: No-one saw me.
           I sneaked in while the orderlies
           Were watching the cup final.

CLIVE: Is this going to catch fire OK?

DAVID: The burning point is eighty, no problem.
            But it burns blue, so it's not so visible.
            It doesn't last very long.

KITTY: It's only to set fire to the straw
            And make a cloud of smoke,
            To gain attention.

DAVID: Thank God for a long hot summer.

CLIVE: Let's hope they can read the words.

DAVID: Planes fly low from Liverpool,
            From Dublin and Belfast.

KITTY: Let's hope they pick it up.
            There's still a free press
            In Europe and the States.

CLIVE: Someone got word to Amsterdam
            Exactly what was happening.
            Netherlands TV got interested,
            They sent a microlight
            With telephoto lenses.

KITTY: I saw a plane with RTF –
            Must have been from France.

DAVID: There's still the United Nations.

[A plane is heard approaching in the distance. It grows in volume.]

KITTY: It's still quite low,
                I think it's Dublin.
                Quick – go pour that stuff
                On the grass,
                Set fire to it.

[DAVID and CLIVE run offstage and do so. KITTY unfolds a large sheet, and as he does so we can read the words 'MURDER HERE' in large home-made letters. He lays it out on the ground. He waves at the plane.]

KITTY: Murder here!

[DAVID and CLIVE join him. A flickering orange light indicates the straw has ignited.]

ALL: [ad lib]   Murder here! Murder here!

[They wave, jump up and down, and point to the banner, as the lights fade to –]

                    BLACKOUT

Scene Fourteen

[ANDREW is holding the hand of his dead partner, who is laid out.]

ANDREW: Well, we did it, mate.
                   Got you to the end,
                   And nobody found out.
                   Maybe we were lucky
                   We didn't realise till late
                   You had the plague.
                   Two short months
                   To live with you dying…
                   I am so glad I stayed with you.
                   I am so glad I shared with you.
                   I never knew how much I loved you
                   Until I knew it could not last.
                   Holding you in my arms,
                   Listening to your rasp of breath…
                   You weighed nothing
                   When I carried you to the loo,
                   Turned you over in the bed,
                   Washed your bed sores,
                   Wiped your arse,
                   Changed the sheets.
                   When you were in pain
                   I massaged you with oils:
                   Tea tree for the skin,
                   And emu oil for your poor joints…
                   You were in so much pain

And all we had was aspirin…
At first I wanted you
To seek some treatment,
But no, you said, dying is private.
There is no cure,
There is no real help,
And this is just between us.

And you were right.
I only wish that you had let me kiss you.

Lying there beside you at the end…
You didn't fight, you said yes to Death,
As you said yes to Life.
You thought of Krishna,
Lord of both.
And when the time was ripe,
You were ready to unloose the chains,
And go…
You taught me how to die;
You taught me how to live.
Now give me strength to bury you.
The undertakers will not touch you
For fear that they will catch it.
They'll cremate you on your own
At the end of the day,
In case you spread disease
To other corpses.

[He tenderly takes the body and tries to carry/drag it off. We

don't know what he is intending to do with it – dump it in a river? Bury it in a wood? Feed it to animals? He is not thinking clearly. He is weak. The lights change, and he is in a harsh spotlight.]

VOICE OFF: *[Gently]* We'll take care of that.
               You're not strong enough,
               You don't know what to do.

ANDREW: You can take me now,
               I don't care.
               I don't regret any of it.
               I'm proud of what I did –
               What we did.
               I'm proud of being gay
               And of our love.

VOICE OFF: Of course you'll have to go
               To the treatment centre.

ANDREW: You think I give a flying fuck
               What happens now?

VOICE OFF: We'll deal with the deceased.
               Are you the next of kin?

ANDREW: His family disowned him,
               I was all he had left.

VOICE OFF: *[As if noting it:]* No next of kin…

[Into a walkie-talkie:] Is there a bin lorry
    in Islington?
Another stiff on Hemingford Estate.

ANDREW: Gerry's not a stiff!
              He was a person,
              Is a person still,
              Living in my mind.
              Treat him with respect;
              Make sure he's buried
              In consecrated ground.

VOICEOVER: That will not be happening –
              Cremation only,
              And covering with quicklime after
              In a communal pit.
              There are too many now.

ANDREW: But he must have consecrated ground –
              He was a priest!

BLACKOUT

Scene Fifteen

[FOWLER's office. A POLICE INSPECTOR. SEBASTIAN, now thin and haggard, sitting opposite. He has a small red spot on the end of his nose.]

INSPECTOR: We've interviewed the staff
At the Newcastle headquarters.
We're sure that none of them
Gave away the codes
To those gay activists.

FOWLER: Can you be sure?

INSP.:   They've taken lie detector tests.
So that leaves only here,
The Ministerial office.

FOWLER: I have the codes of course,
They're locked up in my safe.

INSP.:   And who has access to your safe?

FOWLER: Sebastian,
My personal assistant;
And Sir George,
My permanent secretary.

SEBASTIAN: Excuse me, I'm feeling rather faint –
Would you mind if I opened a window?

FOWLER: Not at all.

[SEBASTIAN gets up unsteadily, and keels over.]

SEBASTIAN: I don't know what's come over me.
             My sense of balance has gone all to pot;
             I think it must be some ear infection.

[He gets to his feet, and immediately collapses again. Gasps for breath. INSPECTOR and FOWLER kneel over him.]

FOWLER: Loosen his clothes –
             Undo his shirt so he can breathe –

INSP.:   Can you take his tie, sir?

[Hands it to FOWLER, who puts it on a chair. INSPECTOR undoes SEBASTIAN's shirt and opens it. When FOWLER turns back he sees a chest covered with lesions.]

FOWLER: Good God! Have you got measles?
             You should see a doctor.

SEBASTIAN: I have seen a doctor.
             I've seen several doctors,
             They're not in any doubt.
             And yes, I'm gay too.

INSP.:   Stand back sir, don't get too close.
             We can't take risks.

SEBASTIAN: I'm sorry, Dad.

[*FOWLER is torn between fear, horror, anger and simple parental love.*]

FOWLER: How long have you had –

SEBASTIAN: About a year, I think.
You remember that fact-finding trip
To Washington DC?
I think I found more than facts.

FOWLER: For god's sake, boy,
Why didn't you tell me?
I'm your father.

SEBASTIAN: How could I?
What would you have done with me?
Off into quarantine?
I know what happens there.

FOWLER: Of course not.
I would have protected you.

SEBASTIAN: One law for the politicians
And one for everyone else.
Think what the press would make of that.

FOWLER: You stupid, selfish child.
You've been putting everyone

At risk.
You've been putting me at risk.

SEBASTIAN: Nobody has been at risk –
Don't you know anything?
Do you think I might have sex with you?

FOWLER: Sebastian!

SEBASTIAN: I'm not an incestophile.
You don't see what is going on
Under your nose.
I came to join you as your P.A.
'To get some work experience'.
I felt so lucky and excited.
Well, I've had experience all right.
Groping, pinching, stroking,
Hand on the thigh,
Hand down the trousers,
From your esteemed colleagues.
Have you any idea how many
Of them are queer?

FOWLER: Well, one or two, I imagine…

SEBASTIAN: Think again.
At least a hundred,
With the House of Lords.
At least one minister has died from GRID –
As we used to call it.

But you don't know…
Doctors collude, the conspiracy of silence,
Call it pneumonia or heart disease.
And what about the heterosexual men,
And carriers with no symptoms?
How do you think the prostitutes all got it?
You think they infected themselves?
I'll bet there's carriers in Westminster.
Most of all it's Honourable Members,
With their honourable diseased members,
Who have the power,
Who have the money,
Who lie to their wives,
Even as they infect them.
They have their careers to think of.
When I started here, I was in awe
Of the excitement and the glamour.
But I have watched the cavalcade of cheats
And hypocrites, who sound off in debates
'Bout family values, moral standards,
And awful promiscuity,
While they walk round led by their cocks
And can't keep it zipped up,
Or have the basic decency
To use a condom.
While we're the scapegoats
For the whole damn thing,
They can go scot free.
Don't you understand, Dad?
You're throwing petrol on the fire.

You punish honesty, reward deceit,
You're wasting money on this quarantine,
It's costing tens of millions
Which could go to research.

INSP.:   You'd better come with me, sir.
Conspiracy's a very serious charge.
So is giving information
Relating to security and intelligence,
Resulting in commission of a crime.

SEBASTIAN: And then the Isle of Man, I suppose?

INSP.:   The judge will decide,
But it's built into the sentence.

FOWLER: No!

INSP.:   It's the law.

SEBASTIAN: The law you piloted through the House
In the teeth of protests –
No evidence at all that it would work –
A sop to the tabloids and your own feral
     pack.
You have brought us all to this, Dad.

[Pause as the enormity of what he has done hits FOWLER.]

FOWLER: What must I do?

SEBASTIAN: Change.
             To change the world,
             First you must change yourself.

*[He puts out his hand for help in getting up. FOWLER over-
comes his instinctive fear and pulls him up. They hug hesit-
antly, then closely.]*

BLACKOUT

Scene Sixteen

[The TV studio again. SEBASTIAN and FOWLER.]

FOWLER: *[Reads, spoken:]* 'Fucking can never be one hundred percent safe, and fucking up the arse is particularly risky, especially for the one getting fucked' – I can't say this, I'm a government minister.

SEBASTIAN: *[Sung:]* That's why you have to say it.
If you can talk about it, anyone can.

FOWLER: I can't see Margaret saying it.
She wanted no mention of gay sex at all.
She thought it would encourage some to do it,
Who'd never even heard of it before.

SEBASTIAN: They used that argument in the House of Lords
About lesbians, in 1921.

FOWLER: Margaret is a child of Queen Victoria
In many many ways.
Though I may talk of it,
Margaret never would.
It would not be ladylike.

SEBASTIAN: Well, almost anyone can mention it.

FOWLER: *[Looks through leaflet again. Spoken:]*
               'Oral sex is not so risky...'
               [Sung:] Funny how I used to think
               Oral sex was whispering obscenities.
               'Taking someone's cock in your mouth' –
               Do men really do this?

SEBASTIAN: Women too.

FOWLER: How many men?

SEBASTIAN: All the gay men I know.

FOWLER: I never knew any of this.

SEBASTIAN: Well, now you do.

[Lights brighten. Cameras are ready. SEBASTIAN straightens his father's tie.]

               Good luck.

FOWLER: You need it more.
               [To camera:]
               I would like to thank the National TV
               For giving me this opportunity
               To say something deeply felt.
               Though I am a government minister,

This is not a government announcement.
There have been too many of those
In recent years,
All based on ignorance,
And I was as ignorant as any.
I want to introduce you
To someone very close and dear to me.
I love him more than anyone in the world
Since my wife died of cancer.
His name is Sebastian, he is my son,
And he has A.I.D.S., as we must call it
now.

[He beckons SEBASTIAN on. They hug intensely. FOWLER ruffles his hair and kisses him on the neck.]

There is as yet no cure for A.I.D.S.,
Although I have tripled the budget for
research.
However, you can minimise your chances
Of being infected by H.I.V.
By taking some precautions.
If you want to fuck –
Yes, I said 'fuck'!
I know it's prime time television
Before the watershed;
I know I'm in the government too,
But I need you all to understand,
Some things are more important
Than your sensibilities.

You'd best get used to it,
You're going to be hearing it a lot.
This is not only for homosexuals,
Everyone should know.
A virus doesn't know who's gay or
    straight.
So together now my lovely son and I
Are going to show you how to use a
    condom.

[SEBASTIAN *produces a banana.*]

I want you to imagine that this is a man's
    prick –
Hasn't he got a big one?

SEBASTIAN: Dad! Stop it!

FOWLER: I'm starting to enjoy being frank.
[*To TV audience:*] You could find it liber-
    ating too.

SEBASTIAN: Now Dad is going to put a rubber on it.

FOWLER: Condom, rubber, johnny, sheath, French
    letter…

[*He produces a condom. Tries to tear it with difficulty; opens
it with his teeth.*]

> Don't worry, it will get a lot easier with
> practice.

[He takes the condom out.]

> Always pinch the end, expel the air,
> And roll it gently down the shaft,
> Until it covers the cock completely.

SEBASTIAN: Of course you can do it
                     Together, with your partner.

FOWLER: If you have any queries,
                Ring the new N.H.S. A.I.D.S. helpline.
                Which is opening after this broadcast
                And will be a twenty-four hour service
                From now on and indefinitely.

SEBASTIAN: And if you're thinking of complaining
                     To the BBC about this broadcast –

BOTH: YOU CAN BUGGER OFF!

[They laugh and hug again.]

BLACKOUT

Scene Seventeen

[SEBASTIAN and FOWLER. SEBASTIAN is blind. FOWLER leads him in.]

SEBASTIAN: Remember now,
I want a party –
A proper Irish wake!
No long faces
And lots of dancing.
I've given you the playlist.

FOWLER: I can't believe you're being so calm.

SEBASTIAN: One of us must be,
And you're a gibbering wreck.

FOWLER: It's all so sudden.

SEBASTIAN: No it's not.
That brain tumour
Was squatting like a toad,
Waiting,
And now it's spat its poison.

FOWLER: But to go blind within a week!
If you'd been seen earlier
We could have spotted it,
Maybe arrested it.
I drove you underground…

I killed you…

SEBASTIAN: Stop this maudlin self-pity.
If I'm not blaming you,
You should not blame yourself.
I've had the time to get used to it.
It's been a good life,
Rich in fun and friends.
I've seen so many die –
And now I'm going to join them.
Not long now –
Get used to it.

FOWLER: A parent should die before his child,
This is unnatural.

SEBASTIAN: 'Unnatural'? How many times have you
used that word?

FOWLER: I know – and now it's ashes in my mouth.

SEBASTIAN: I take that back.
No more guilt! Be gone, dull care!
I'd ask for champagne
If I could still swallow.

FOWLER: You'll have the best of treatment,
That I promise you.

SEBASTIAN: There is no treatment,

I'm resigned to that.

FOWLER: No! Never resigned!
            We have to fight this thing.
            I owe it to you,
            I owe it to poor old Boofie.
            The treatment centre
            Will become just that:
            The best of medical attention,
            Nutrition, comfort, and respect.
            And anyone can leave who wishes to,
            We will help them.

SEBASTIAN: *[Ironic]* Really? We, the government?
            There have been too many promises and
                lies.

FOWLER: How can I not do this?
            I'll make it my life's work,
            I have to do it for you.

BLACKOUT

Scene Eighteen

[A ferry hooter; seagulls. On the dock of Douglas, Isle of Man.
KITTY and DAVID are waiting.]

KITTY: Look, the ferry's coming.
It's been a constant to-and-fro
All week, and still there's more
To rehabilitate.
It will be strange to go home.

DAVID: If we can still call it home.
All the people who spat at us,
Who shouted for us to be put away,
Who painted 'Pouf' and 'Plague' on our
    front doors,
The oh-so-helpful neighbours,
Who turned their backs on us in the
    street.

KITTY: There are laws now to protect us.

DAVID: Yes, I know. And grants to compensate us.
I know people whose houses were burnt
    down
By mobs with flaming torches.
Do you think the mobs will change
Because the government tells them to?

KITTY: They will change in time.

DAVID: And more will die in time.
                Like Clive.
                I wish he'd lived to see this.
                I miss him so.

KITTY: There is no magic wand.
                We must have time…

*[Split stage. FOWLER enters with SCIENTIST. They study a
print-out.]*

SCIENTIST: As you can see, this chart shows
                That when the drug is given to rats,
                It inhibits the enzyme reverse tran-
                    scriptase.

FOWLER: In English, please.

SCIENTIST: It appears to stabilise the t-cells…

FOWLER: … Which help the other white blood cells
                To boost immunity.

SCIENTIST: Correct. The upshot is,
                The rats that took the drug
                On average lived some months more
                Than other rats with the infection.

FOWLER: But still they died.

SCIENTIST: Yes, but it's a start;
              Perhaps in combination
              With other drugs…

FOWLER: What is this drug called?

SCIENTIST: Zidovudine. It was intended to prevent
              Mothers passing viruses to babies.
              At the moment it's the best we have,
              And in time –

FOWLER: There is no time.
              My son is dead.
              We have no time.

KITTY/DAVID: We have no time.

DAVID: My Clive is dead.

SCIENTIST: At the moment time is all we have –

FOWLER: We have wasted so much time.

KITTY/DAVID: We have waited far too long.

FOWLER/KITTY/DAVID:
              So many died who didn't have to,
              From apathy and bigotry
              Ignorance and fear.

SCIENTIST: We need time…
              Trust in us,
              Trust in science.

KITTY/DAVID: No, trust ourselves,
                To make connections –

FOWLER: To work together –

KITTY/DAVID: To help each other –

FOWLER: For the sake of the dead –

KITTY/DAVID: To organise ourselves –

FOWLER/SCIENTIST: To tell the truth –

FOWLER: To calm the fears –

KITTY/DAVID: By being ourselves –

ALL: To calm the fears –

SCIENTIST: To find a cure,
              We need time…

ALL: Though there is no time,
        We yet need time…
        Time…
        Time.

BLACKOUT

THE END

A Gay Century: 14

1986: A Shot at the Future

Travels with a turkey baster

Above: *Lesbian parents*
Below: *Gay parents*

Introduction

Some lesbians have always had babies: by their husbands, by male friends, by anonymous donors. Certainly, sexuality doesn't seem to dampen what is dubiously known as the 'maternal instinct' for many. Gay men have been known to get broody too.

It was in the latter part of the 1970s that lesbian parenting came to national prominence. At that time, lesbian mothers who had children in heterosexual relationships were very liable to lose their children if the fathers fought the mothers for custody. Being a lesbian made them inherently unsuitable mothers, said judges. But many men were either more enlightened, or more reluctant to shoulder the responsibility, and as a result many lesbians went into new relationships with children from previous marriages. One such was Babs Todd, who brought three children to her relationship with Jackie Forster. Together in 1972 they founded Sappho, a lesbian social group and *Sappho*, a monthly magazine for lesbians to replace the old *Arena 3*.

At Sappho meetings they entertained many lesbians who wanted to have children, and found a doctor who was prepared to offer Artificial Insemination by Donor [A.I.D.] This despite the official N.H.S. line that it was only available to heterosexual married couples. A national tabloid newspaper got hold of this story, boiled with righteous indignation that lesbians were availing themselves of this technique while so many so-called 'normal' women were childless, and Jackie and the pioneering doctor were hung out to dry. It was not until the late 1990s that A.I.D. was made available on the N.H.S. for unmarried women or same-sex couples.

However, the issue did not go away. By the 1980s more lesbians were having children than ever before, but taking the matter into their own hands, literally. Most commonly, a woman would find a close friend, often gay, and ask him to be the father of her child. In sensible arrangements, the rules of engagement were laid out carefully. Would there be intercourse, or use of a turkey baster? Would the father have a role to play in upbringing? Or support? Would the child be told who their father was, and if so, when? In other cases, it was more haphazard, with traumatic consequences.

It is nowadays axiomatic that anyone wanting to be a father will be subject to a battery of tests for medical conditions, including A.I.D.S./H.I.V. In 1985–86 it was difficult for a gay man wanting to conceive with a lesbian woman to go along to his G.P. and talk the matter through, let alone arrange a hospital visit. There was a test for H.I.V. antibodies, ELISA[6], but results were nothing like 100% accurate, and the test kit itself came with a health warning on the label, 'It is inappropriate to use this test as a screen for A.I.D.S., or as a screen for members of groups at increased risk for A.I.D.S. in the general population.' In any case, you were reluctant to take a test which might be inaccurate, and even if accurate could offer no hope of

---

[6] Enzyme-Linked Immuno-Sorbent Assay, developed for other purposes in the early 1970s.

treatment. As a result, many couples were threshing around in a medical and moral vacuum, caught between conflicting desires.

I was asked to father the child of a lesbian friend in 1986, and went to America for the purpose. Some of this experience is reflected in the play, but I must absolutely emphasise that this is not an autobiographical piece.

Because it is an opera libretto, the story is simplified; the outcomes and the dynamics are changed. The piece needed a strong storyline to work within the structure Robert and I set ourselves, which life did not supply. In the libretto each parent has a partner, neither of whom really wants the child, though for different reasons. One scene however is lifted straight from life, which is the father, Perry's, monologue as he is trying to ejaculate into a petri dish for Lou's benefit. One of my friends who went through a similar hoop commented on the 'Brian-Rixness of it all'. I think 'The Masturbation Aria' must be some kind of first, but I doubt if it will become a staple of operatic recitals. I have also, particularly in the opening twenty minutes, tried to reflect on the multiple meanings we give to babies and parenthood, and how those meanings reflect our ego and our inadequacies. Mini-Me lives on, despite our better intentions.

A Shot in the Future is set at a very precise moment in time, 1986, and in a precise place, Coventry. In the gradual accumulation of knowledge and awareness about H.I.V. / A.I.D.S., the gay community had always been ahead of the curve, thanks to the pioneering educative work of the weekly freesheet, *Capital Gay*, and the formation of the

Terrence Higgins Trust. Lesbian and Gay Switchboard, as it was then, also spread enlightenment; it had come a long way since the days when its safe sex advice consisted of 'Don't Sleep with Americans.' However, we were still at the stage when there was only recently an agreed term for the virus, an erratic test for it, and no sign of a vaccine or cure. There are still no vaccines or cures, despite the passage of nearly forty years and 32,000,000 deaths.

If you lived outside London in 1986, even comparatively well-informed lesbian and people might well not have understood the full implications of H.I.V./A.I.D.S., particularly in regard to parenting. The Department of Health had only recently banned gay men from giving blood, a ban many denounced as pure homophobia; some gay men ignored the ban, relying on their own judgement of the personal risk they offered.

Because of this, the attitudes of the characters in this scenario are consistent with their possible state of knowledge at this time and in this place.

Originally, I intended *Quarantine* to be the only full-length piece in the cycle, because of the importance of the subject to our world-view. However, I was up against a deadline. In March 2020 I announced that we would be doing on-line Zoom readings of the entire cycle, despite the fact that three plays were as yet unwritten. I calculated that the weekly readings would take a total of just over two months, and I could write the missing plays [*The Berlin Boy*, *A Shot at the Future*, and *Two into One*] during the run. In the event, they took about two weeks each, and it remains a truism of writing that it is easier and quicker to produce something to a longer word length than to a shorter. In fact, the shorter the piece is to be, the longer it takes. At one point, with the deadline looming, I cheated by incorporating the lyric of a lullaby I had written previously to music by the talented Hungarian composer and another regular collaborator, Matyas Bascó.

Whether this accounts for the comparative length of *A Shot at the Future;* or whether the story simply needed longer to be told in all its complexity, to do justice to all four viewpoints, I don't know. I hope it doesn't outstay its welcome.

CAST

BEVERLEY, KNOWN AS BEV: Mezzo-Soprano
Early 30s. A brisk new barrister, a high flyer used to proving she's as good as, or better than, men. She keeps a large Alsatian, Sheba.

LUCY, KNOWN AS LOU: Soprano
Late 30s. Bev's lover, and rather dominated by her. She is a writer, and given to living in a world of her own.

PERICLES, KNOWN AS PERRY: Baritone
Early 30s. Lou's best friend, also a writer, but an only child, so rather stubborn and self-centred. From a Greek family long-time resident in Britain, he retains a certain Mediterranean volatility.

PHILIP, KNOWN AS FLIP: Tenor
Early 20s. Perry's boyfriend; this is his first serious relationship, and he's very committed to it. He values the security, having been badly treated during his childhood and rejected at his coming out. He is very handsome, and something of a trophy to Perry.

SETTING

The play is set in the West Midlands. Flexible, multi-scene. A bed as part of it, which serves as both the boys' and the girls' bedrooms [different covers]. There is a pram in a corner, in which a doll [the baby] is kept. The doll is brought out as a prop.

INSTRUMENTS

Piano trio: piano, violin, cello.

A SHOT AT THE FUTURE

ACT ONE

Scene One

[The four actors stand at the corners of the stage, unaware of each other. This mirrors the set-up for '1936: Fishing'.]

BEV: *[Dubious:]* A baby...

LOU: *[Dreamy:]* A baby...

PERRY: *[Wondering:]* A baby...?

FLIP: *[Aghast:]* A baby!

[BEV and LOU move into the scene, PERRY and FLIP exit.]

Duet

LOU: I've always wanted a baby.
                  I come from a Catholic family,
                  Outrageously fertile.
                  Seven siblings, ten nephews, eight nieces.
                  I feel I'll let the side down
                  If I don't spawn.

BEV: Don't joke about it,
                  It's a serious matter.

You know how hard I work,
I'm exhausted as it is,
Running to stand still.
I'd never be able to work
At home in the evenings.
It would ruin your writing.
The pram in the hall,
The mortal enemy of art.

LOU: I don't believe that.
                I can look after a sprog
                And write as well.
                It will take after me –
                Very independent.
                Anyway, you can help –

BEV: I can help?
                I'm out all day,
                I earn the money
                To keep us comfortable –
                To keep you comfortable.
                I can't do any more.

* * *

[She lights a cigarette.]

LOU: *[At the cigarette:]* Do you have to?

BEV: Yes!

LOU: Outside perhaps?

BEV: I'm under a lot of stress.
      Know what I think?
      All this has happened
      Since you started going down
      To London, and to Sappho.

LOU: I've only been a few times.

BEV: Since you met Jackie Forster
      And her pussy posse,
      You've been all broody.

LOU: Don't use that word!

BEV: Why not?
      A lot of women go through this.
      There were other women too
      At the Sappho meetings
      With children.

LOU: Fighting for custody of them!
      Courts say lesbians are unfit mothers.
      We'll prove them wrong.

BEV: You know what I think this is?
      Competitive spirit.
      If other women have them,
      You must too.

LOU: One, only one.

BEV: I know you. You say that now,
            But then it will be,
            'Two are just as easy as one,
            And just as cheap to keep'.
            Like they were dogs.

LOU: Those other women aren't like us.
            Their children are leftovers
            From their marriages.
            Don't you see? This will be our child.
            Not yours, but ours.
            Think, Bev, love,
            Someone we can mould and shape,
            Who will follow us, our legacy,
            Our shot at the future.

BEV: There's only one problem –
            I don't have a maternal bone in my body.

LOU: You'll come to love her,
            I know you will.

BEV: Her? Are you sure?

LOU: I even know her name.
            Billie, as in Holiday,
            Or Billie Jean King.
            [Intimate:] Oh Bev, can't you see?

It can only make us stronger,
You and I together.
It will pull us closer –
Lately we have drifted.

BEV: That's true.

LOU: We can be a family.

[BEV has been smoking furiously. She stubs the cigarette out.]

LOU: You'll have to give those up.
           Bad for baby's health.

BEV: You're so self-righteous
           Since you gave them up yourself.
           I hate that 'baby'. Sentiment.
           'The baby', for God's sake.
           And where will we put it?

LOU: *Her* – I hope –

BEV: The baby – where? Where?

LOU: We'll find room. Or move.

BEV: Look, Lou, I know how you think.
           'I'm thirty-eight;
           If I don't do it soon,
           It will be too late.'

In ten years' time
You'll have a surge of guilt.

LOU: It's more than that.

BEV: You will, you will –
You'll know you can never be a mother,
So you can't be a real woman.

LOU: Don't you want it too?
After all, now you know –

BEV: Know that I can't have children?
That's right. Spell it out.
Rub it in.

LOU: That's why you and Tom split up.

BEV: Oh no. That's why Tom split up.
I was glad to go my own way,
And find myself.
[She takes LOU's hand.]
Look, love, I understand
How much you feel.
I went through much the same
When my mother died.
I wanted one so much.
I didn't know I couldn't –
Thank the Lord.

LOU: You're only saying that.
              Why can't we have a child?

BEV: Because I live with you.
              I like my life.
              I like order,
              I like our flat,
              And I love you.
              I won't let anything change that,
              Even for you.

LOU: Nothing needs to change.

[Lights fade leaving LOU in a single spot. BEV steps away. It is LOU's imagination, so soft lights. LOU goes to the cot and brings it out to centre stage. There is a life-size baby doll in it. She takes it out, gently takes off its clothes, produces a sponge and gently soaps the doll.]

Aria

LOU: Flesh of my flesh,
              You were an easy birth.
              I felt you ease from me,
              Slippery as a fish.
              Your little hands grasp my finger,
              A grip so strong,
              Soft and strong.
              Everything about you is so perfect,
              From the tiny nails

On your tiny toes,
To the little tongue,
Which you stick out
To catch more milk
From the nipples
Of my full breasts.
As I wash you,
Your skin so soft,
Your flesh so frail,
Your bones so delicate,
I can smell you, baby,
Baby, baby.
Nothing but baby everywhere,
Milky and sweet.
Even your baby poo is sweet,
As I tenderly unwrap the nappy
Turn you over, take it out from under.

[Does the action, turns the doll over]

There you go,
Wipe your bottom.
You look at me
With eyes so trusting.
Mummy Lou is here for you,
Mummy Lou will shelter you.

[She takes a new nappy, puts powder on it. Does up the nappy.]

Billie, you are rare and precious,
Best thing in my life.
I hold you close,
So close.

*   *   *

[BEV comes into the scene, into the dream, puts her hand on
LOU's shoulder.]

LOU: Even if I cannot have Bev to wife,
                Yet we are strong in love,
                When one plus one makes three.

BEV/LOU: Lou and Bev will shelter you,
                Your two mummies –

BEV: And no daddy –

BEV/LOU: We will keep you safe from harm.
                We will clothe you,
                Keep you warm.
                You will always be
                Cosy at the centre
                Of our family.

[They exchange a look of love. LOU gets the clothes and they
dress the baby together. They sing a vocalise lullaby to it. It is
impossibly romantic. The lights fade as they lay the baby in the
cot and return it to the corner.]

[Lights change. They are back in the scene. BEV is there again.]

BEV: Are you really so serious?

LOU: Darling, I am aching.

BEV: Are you sure you can cope?
            It's a big step.

LOU: The biggest!

BEV: And what about your work? Your writing?
            Remember Cyril Connolly:
            'There is no greater enemy of art
            Than the pram in the hall.'

LOU: That was just a cover-up,
            Because he couldn't hack it.
            Preferred to socialise,
            Supported by his wife.

BEV: I support you.

LOU: But I still work.

BEV: Will you still work?

LOU: I'll give myself maternity leave.

BEV: I'll never get maternity leave.
My chambers don't know that I'm...
They can never know.

LOU: A baby will be very awkward...
How do you explain it?

BEV: I won't have to.
I won't be the one who's pregnant.

LOU: And later?

BEV: They won't need to know.

LOU: Are you ashamed of me?
Are you?

BEV: No. No.

LOU: That's why we've been having arguments.
I've put up with the burden of your shame
For the sake of your career –
But I'm damned if my baby will!

BEV: Our baby –

LOU: 'Our'? That's a change of tune.
Do you really mean that? Think...

BEV: If – I say if – we have the baby,

I will tell my chambers
About her, and about you.
I promise.
And I'll help the best I can.
But how on earth to manage?
You have a contract with your publisher;
They want another Molly Miller story
Sometime next year –
You can't just stop.
There's the mortgage to pay,
It devours everything we earn,
Both of us.

LOU: There's always nurseries.

BEV: More expense.
And what about a father?
Clinics cost money too.
It can take months –
Years, even.

LOU: You know very well,
I.V.F. is for married couples –
Heterosexual couples.
No wedding ring? No petri dish,
No incubator.
But there is another way;
I was thinking – Perry…?

BEV: *[Horrified]* Perry?

LOU: I don't mean, doing it with him.
               I thought he might donate his sperm.
               I've known him all my life,
               Since we were both
               In Bluecoats Grammar School.
               He was the first person
               I told that I was gay,
               Then I found out
               That he was gay as well.
               He's sensible and stable,
               He dotes on that little niece of his.
               Fatherhood would suit him.

[She turns, BEV leaves. PERRY comes in.]

Scene Two

[PERRY and LOU are walking in a park. Sounds of ducks and park noises.]

LOU: Fatherhood would suit you.

PERRY: A baby?

LOU: Why not?

PERRY: But why me?
'Of all the penises
In all the towns
In all the world
You walk into mine.'

LOU: Eew!
Not your penis,
You smug man.
I'm certainly not walking
Into your penis.
I need your sperm.
Your penis is a necessary means
To a desired end

Canon

PERRY: If a baby is desired,
Then a penis is required.

LOU: It's your sperm that is desired,
           If a baby would be sired.

PERRY: My penis must be hired.
           If some sperm should be acquired.

[This is a little canon, and repeats – the sort of game they play together.]

LOU: Hired? I'm not paying, you bastard.

PERRY: It was only for the rhyme.

LOU: Don't you see? You'd make a wonderful
           father.

PERRY: Really?

LOU: You're cute and funny –

PERRY: *[Bashful]* Aw shucks!

LOU: I'm serious.
           You're bright and gentle,
           You're my best friend in all the world.
           You have everything I want my child to
           have.
           I want it to have the best.

PERRY: You sure know how to flatter a girl.

LOU: With your intelligence, my talent –

PERRY: Or my athletic skill, your looks –

[*They look at each other.*]

BOTH: No way!

PERRY: [*Genuinely tentative*] I don't know how to
                   put this, but –

LOU: A sterilised bowl and a turkey baster.

PERRY: I don't have a turkey baster.
                   I'm a vegetarian.

LOU: We buy a turkey baster, idiot.
                   They're two pounds in Woolworth's.

PERRY: That's not very sexy.

LOU: That's hardly the point.

PERRY: And what does Bev think about this?

LOU: She'll come round to it –
                   She's starting to come round already.
                   She'll want it because I want it.

PERRY: And you really want it?

LOU: Really, really.

PERRY: Really, really, really, really, really?

LOU: You betcha.

PERRY: And can I be a father? A real father?

LOU: Classic case of a new man.
            Baby carrier wrap in front,
            Talking with the mummies
            Outside playgroup.

[Lights fade leaving PERRY in a single spot. We are in his fantasy of being a father. He is holding a larger doll – a toddler – who is staggering forward with his support.]

Aria

PERRY: Hold on to daddy,
            Take daddy's hand.
            You can do it…
            What a strong boy!
            One step – and again –
            Yes! Aren't you clever!
            Just like your Daddy.

[He looks in the doll's eyes.]

            You got your daddy's eyes,

And his chin, and his hair.
Now walk with me –

[Calls off.] Hey, Flip! Come here!
Billy's walking –
My boy is walking!
He's done three steps!
Flip!

* * *

[FLIP, PERRY's boyfriend, runs in.]

FLIP: Let me see!

[PERRY walks the doll forward.]

FLIP: Wow! That's amazing!

PERRY: Isn't it?

FLIP: To think he's only ten months old.

PERRY: He's turning into quite the little man.

FLIP: Like Daddy.

PERRY: You think so?

FLIP: Just like Daddy.

253

He's going to be as cute as Daddy.

BOTH: And you will be so lucky,
Growing up with two Daddies
Of your very own.

[They embrace, holding the doll between them.]

FLIP: We'd better take Billy back to his Mummy.
Does Billy want to go back to his Mummy?
Yes, he does. Yes he does.
[To PERRY:]
I'll take him back to Lou,
You put the supper on.

[He exits with doll. PERRY turns back into the scene, lights change, LOU is there again.]

PERRY: A baby?
The idea grows on me.
What are you looking for?
A donor?
Wham, bam, thank-you Sam?
I'd find that hard –
I'd be too curious.
Are you expecting – even – love?

LOU: I'm not a man-hater,
I wouldn't ask you if I was.
I would want you to be part of his life.

You would want that, wouldn't you?

PERRY:　　　I'd certainly be curious.

LOU:　　　Perry, don't you see?
It could be wonderful.
Two mothers and two fathers –
What better mentors could it have?
You'll take Billie for the weekend,
And for holidays –
Maybe more if we both need a break.
No-one exhausted,
Everyone with another life.

PERRY:　　　I'll take Billy to the zoo –

LOU:　　　Please, no zoos,
Zoos are cruel.

PERRY:　　　OK, to the ecopark.
We'll go fishing –

LOU:　　　That's cruel too –

PERRY:　　　*[Sighing]* Okay…

LOU:　　　Football in the winter,
Cricket in the summer.

PERRY:　　　I hate cricket.

LOU: OK, swimming, then.

PERRY: We can both do swimming.

LOU: And I will do the tennis.

PERRY: A baby…
           And we can have a dog too.

LOU: Yes!
           Another dog like ours.

PERRY: I'll have an excuse
           To go to all the Disney movies –
           'Pinocchio', 'Dumbo',
           'Lady and the Tramp',
           And to see the new ones too –
           'The Fox and the Hound'.

LOU: Only think –
           A whole young life takes shape
           In front of you!

PERRY: Yes…
           To pass on all your knowledge
           With your DNA.
           No-one wants to be forgotten
           When they go.

LOU: Don't talk like that.

Aria

PERRY: We all must go.
Sometimes you wonder…
You imagine your own funeral;
You wonder if anyone
Will write your obituary,
And what it will read like.
If. Are you that important?
And then you start to ask:
Who will remember me? For what?
Flip will remember me, of course.
But even he won't last for ever.

LOU: Nothing lasts forever. Not even a baby.

PERRY: But you've left something,
Made a mark.
The river of your DNA flows on.
You've passed a torch –
I don't know, I can't explain.

* * *

LOU: Sometimes I see the babies
In pushchairs at the supermarket.
I know exactly why
Other women steal them.
My breasts get heavy with longing –
It is very physical.

My whole body is crying out
For a baby.

PERRY: Sounds like a classic case.

LOU: Funny how it gets some women
But not others.
Bev is just the opposite.

PERRY: Lucky Bev. Self-contained.

LOU: She wouldn't be successful
If she wasn't self-contained.

PERRY: I could almost envy her.

LOU: We're different, that's all.
I was made to change nappies
From a very early age –
All those siblings.

PERRY: I could get into nappies.

LOU: They wouldn't suit you.

PERRY: I mean, changing nappies.

LOU: I had to make up lunch boxes –

PERRY: And making lunch boxes –

BOTH: And worry when it starts to get dark.

LOU: And Flip? Can we count on him?

BOTH: I wonder what Flip will say…

[Lights fade on them. A very short instrumental break to allow time to change the cover on the bed, and maybe put up some marker of masculinity.]

Scene Three

[PERRY and FLIP's flat. Evening.]

FLIP: A baby?

PERRY: Yes, a baby.
               I'm going to be a father.
               Why not?

FLIP: Are you crazy?

PERRY: What's so terrible?

FLIP: You mean you're really going to screw her?

PERRY: Don't be crude. There are other ways…

FLIP: You mean into a test tube?
               Like some prize bull?

PERRY: What's wrong with that?
               Hundreds do it every year…
               I do believe you're jealous.

FLIP: It's inhuman, darling. Mechanical.

PERRY: And this from the boy
               I found in the Subway Club,
               In a gang-bang in the dark

With his trousers round his ankles.

FLIP: That's different.
That's sex, not *[sneering]* reproduction.

PERRY: You say that it's inhuman.
It *will* be human, that's the point.
It's Lou, my oldest friend.
I feel honoured that she's chosen me.
We've talked a lot,
We've got it all worked out;
We'll share responsibility.
And the expense.

FLIP: And the time. Don't forget the time.
Babies take an awful lot of time –
I'll never see you on your own.
Every time we want some sex,
That squalling brat will put a stop to it.
Why don't you marry her
While you're about it?

PERRY: Don't be crass.
You have a nasty streak
Of misogyny
I never recognised before.

FLIP: Can I be honest?

PERRY: Of course.

FLIP: Cards on the table?

PERRY: Try me.

FLIP: I don't want the responsibility.

PERRY: Ok, it's *my* responsibility,
             Not yours.

FLIP: Just how do you propose
             To separate the two things out,
             Fatherhood and – er – loverhood?
             If it comes to stay,
             What am *I* meant to do?
             Move out for the weekend?

PERRY: I'll look after it.
             You can help look after it.

FLIP: And what if I don't want to
             Help to look after it?
             It won't choose who to wake
             When it cries out in the night.
             Once you're out cold
             You could sleep through a rape alarm.
             Use your brain:
             What do we do at the weekend?
             We go out, right?
             We go to pictures,
             We eat in restaurants,

We dance at discos.
Sometimes we get laid.

PERRY: We can manage both.

FLIP: The sprog can tag along? Ha!
I don't think that a baby sling
Will match your skimpy spandex shorts.

[The lights fade down and PERRY goes to lie on the bed. Single spot on him. We are in FLIP's fantasy. FLIP joins him. The DOLL/CHILD is up against the wall, just out of sight. It looks at them. The next section is mainly action. FLIP and PERRY start making out. FLIP is very stilted, aware of the child. After a while, PERRY stops, protests:]

PERRY: What's the matter?
What's eating you?

FLIP: Billy's watching me, I know he is.

PERRY: All he'll see is two loving men,
He won't know anything else.
He should get used to it.

FLIP: I don't like it.

[He gets up, takes the doll, and turns it to the wall.]

FLIP: Now, go to sleep –

And no peeping.
This is not for little boys.

[He goes back to PERRY. They start again, and PERRY's love-making becomes more excited and noisy. FLIP starts feeling inhibited again.]

PERRY: What now?

FLIP: He'll hear us. He'll hear *you*.

PERRY: No he won't.

FLIP: The walls are paper thin.

PERRY: What's wrong with the sound of love?

FLIP: The noise you make, he'll think I'm
                hurting you.

PERRY: I should be so lucky.

FLIP: Will you be serious?
                Do you realise what you sound like?
                A bull in pain.

PERRY: You said you liked the noise I make –
                You said it turned you on.

FLIP: Not with Billy listening.

PERRY: How do you know he's listening?
                He's probably fast asleep.

FLIP: Do you want to wake him up?

PERRY: No

FLIP: Then – quietly –

[They start to make out again. PERRY automatically calls out, FLIP puts a hand over his mouth. This time PERRY stops and pushes off.]

PERRY: It's no use. I've lost it.

[He gets up, puts his clothes on.]

PERRY: I'm going to sleep on the sofa
                In the living room.

[He exits. FLIP still has an erection – he is a healthy, randy young man. He tries to turn over and go to sleep, but it is very uncomfortable. He turns on his back, and starts to masturbate, as the lights fade to BLACKOUT. When they come up again, PERRY is dressed and back in the present, putting on his coat. Calls to FLIP.]

PERRY: Hurry up, we'll miss the start of the film.

FLIP: I'm coming.

PERRY: It's got some gorgeous boys in it –
            Rupert Everett, Colin Firth –

FLIP: Never heard of them.

PERRY: Take my word for it.

FLIP: *[Appearing fully dressed:]* Alright, already.
            We won't be able to go out like this
            After we get the baby.

PERRY: Lou and Bev can babysit.

FLIP: If it's our turn to have him?

PERRY: We can take him with us.

FLIP: To *Another Country?*
            Certificate fifteen?
            How do you think he'd pass?
            Put a moustache on him
            In his carrycot?
            You're off your head!

PERRY: Well, maybe not…
            We'll play with him, then.
            The films will wait.
            But not this one… Come on.

[He tries to take FLIP's hand, but FLIP is abstracted and

doesn't take it.]

[FADE to BLACK. A short instrumental break to feminise the bedroom]

Scene Four

[BEV and LOU in bed. BEV has her glasses on, looking severe and lawyerly. She is reading a brief. LOU is writing her novel in a notebook.]

BEV: Lou?

LOU: Mmm...?

BEV: *[Louder]* Lou!

LOU: What?

BEV: Sorry to interrupt your concentration.

LOU: I was on a roll.

BEV: Would you scratch my back, please?

LOU: *[Putting book down, resigned:]* Sure. *[She does so.]*
     What are you working on?

BEV: You'll be interested. It's a suit for defamation.
     The Evening Telegraph is saying
     The council leader's gay.
     And in election year!

LOU: Well – Isn't he?

BEV: That's not the point.
            To call someone gay publicly
            Is defamatory.

LOU: Only if you think being gay
            Is inferior.

BEV: The law does,
            The judges and the courts do:
            It's a character defect, or weakness.

LOU: I thank the Lord
            For my character defect,
            Which I hope I will pass on to my child.

BEV: Are you serious?
            The children of most lesbians turn out
                straight.
            Just wait: she'll bring her boyfriends
            Home to meet her mummies.

LOU: Are you serious?

BEV: Are you?
            If you're doing this to make a little dyke –
            Forget it.

LOU: Repeat to self:

A child is not an extension of me.
It will be an independent person.

BEV: You're still set on it?

LOU: Never more serious –
And Perry's up for it too.

BEV: Perry is a fantasist.
You're two small children
Playing at mummies and daddies.
It will get real soon enough,
When you're exhausted from lack of sleep,
And your nipples are raw
From the constant suck.

*[During this last speech, LOU slips out of bed and puts the doll
near the bed in the cot. Scatters some of BEV's papers on the
floor. Exits. Lights change. This is now BEV's fantasy. BEV
trying to concentrate. A child's cry.]*

BEV: *[Calling:]* Lou! *[Child cries more.]* Lou!
Can you deal with this?

[She sees the papers on the floor.]

Aria

Oh, Billie, look what you've done.

270

[She gets out of bed and starts scrabbling amongst them.]

How am I to find anything ever again?

[The child starts crying again. BEV holds the doll quite roughly.]

Shut up! Shut up!
Don't you know I'm in court tomorrow?
No, of course you don't.
You're just a machine to eat, piss and shit.

[A fart –]

And fart. *[She waves the toxic smell away.]*
  Oh, God.
I haven't had a decent sleep in months.
I'm run ragged.
I have to work twice as hard
As male barristers,
Just to get a level hearing.
And you – you –
You don't care, do you?
As long as you get your Heinz baby food –
Which you then vomit over my clean
  blouse.
You want to know the bottom line, Billie?
I don't like you. I can't stand you.
Some days I could strangle you.
Many days –

271

Every day I could strangle you.
When am I going to have
Some space to concentrate?
When am I going to get some peace?

[She looks at the assorted papers in bewilderment. Pulls herself together.]

You are woman, you are strong.

* * *

[The baby starts crying again.]

Barristers don't have babies
Barristers have nannies!
Lou! Lou!

LIGHTS FADE TO BLACKOUT

Scene Five

[FLIP and BEV looking in the window of Mothercare.]

FLIP: Are you going to have to get all this stuff?

BEV: That's what Lou is saying.
             Not all of it, just a bit of it.
             Some clothes, some toys, a pram –

FLIP: Look at the prices of the prams!
             Two hundred and fifty pounds!

BEV: She thinks I can afford it.
             I subsidise her writing,
             I'll subsidise her baby.
             That's the way her scatty logic goes:
             'The briefs are coming in,
             She can afford it.'
             That's the way she thinks.
             But there's the overdraft
             From all the early years,
             And the mortgage.
             She doesn't think of that.
             The average child
             Costs seventy-five thousand pounds
             To raise to age eighteen.
             And that's before University!

FLIP: Have you told her that?

BEV: She knows that they're expensive.

FLIP: You could always get second hand…

BEV: A second hand child?!

FLIP: A second hand pram.

BEV: She'd never have that –
            Nothing but the best for her.
            And then there's status.
            I'm not having other mums
            Looking down their noses at Billie
            For being badly dressed,
            Or in a battered old pram.
            Having lesbian parents is hard enough
            Without that awful mumsy snobbery.

FLIP: Look at those cute blue romper suits!

BEV: Glad to see you breaking down
            The gender stereotypes.
            None of this 'blue for a boy' nonsense.

FLIP: What do you mean?
            Blue *is* for a boy.
            Perry told me his name is Billy!

BEV: Oh, no. *Her* name is Billie.
            B-I-L-L-I-E. As in Holiday.

FLIP: What makes you think
           It's going to be a girl?

BEV: Lou's convinced it will be.

FLIP: How can she know?

BEV: She's set her heart on it.
           She only ever talks of her.

FLIP: *[Trying to keep a note of triumph out of his
               voice:]*
           You know the chances of having a girl
           Are about four to one against?

BEV: What rubbish you talk! It has to be 50–50.
           Where did you get that from?

FLIP: I read it somewhere. Or someone told me.
           I can't remember which.

BEV: *[Sarcastic]* Well that makes it gospel truth!

FLIP: Don't you see it in the playgroups?
           Haven't you been with lesbian mothers?
           Most of them have boys.
           It's what happens with A.I.D.
           When you have a normal fuck
           To try and have a baby,
           Your semen bursts with male sperm.

275

On their way to the egg,
More of the boys drop out,
Because we're weaker.

BEV: Brother, you said it.

FLIP: Leaving a fifty-fifty ratio.
             But when the end of the turkey baster
             Goes up against the cervix
             Straight to the fallopian tube –
             Little wriggly boy sperm everywhere.

[This is said with a kind of triumph. BEV is stunned, beginning to be convinced.]

BEV: How come you know this, and I don't?

FLIP: I thought you would.
             I'm surprised you don't.
             Haven't you talked it over with Lou?
             'What if it's a boy'?

BEV: No... we never really did.
             Her broodiness suppressed
             All other thoughts.

FLIP: How can a women-only house
             Have a male child?

BEV: You really don't want this child, do you?

FLIP: Do you?

BEV: No. I'm scared of losing Lou
               If she has it.
               I'm scared of losing her if she doesn't.
               And I'm jealous.

FLIP: I'm scared of losing Perry.

BOTH: We really have to stop it.

               FADE TO BLACKOUT

               END OF ACT ONE

ACT TWO

Scene Six:

[LOU and PERRY in the Park again.]

LOU: Are you getting second thoughts?

PERRY: It's not that, exactly,
But suddenly it all seems very difficult.
At first it seemed like fun,
Now it looks a lot more like hard work.

LOU: A lot of it is hard work.

PERRY: And Flip is being difficult.

LOU: He'll come round. Bev is coming round.

PERRY: I know so little about it.
I'm reading books,
The Pregnancy Service pamphlets.
Such a strange and alien world.

LOU: 'Mothers from Mars' – the movie.
Look, I'm sure all parents feel like that
The first time.

PERRY: I know so little about women's bodies.
I don't know that much about my own!

LOU: You don't need to.
            The clinic will take care of it,
            Tell you what you need to know.

PERRY: Which clinic?

LOU: The Pregnancy Advice Service,
            The one in Upper Hill Street.

PERRY: Oh, you mean the one
            Where Right-to-Lifers give you
            Leaflets saying you're a murderer,
            And spit at you as you go by.

LOU: I'll protect you.

PERRY: Don't joke. They could make you miscarry.

LOU: I'm still going. I've set my mind on it.
            Besides there's the antenatal classes –

PERRY: Do you have to go to classes?
            Will I be allowed to go to classes?

LOU: Why not? You're the father.

PERRY: The gay father –

LOU: Everyone will know that anyway!
            No straight father would go

To antenatal classes. It's too girly.
And I'm the gay mother,
They're used to it.
You must get used to it as well.

PERRY: You know the thought I can't get from
        my head?

LOU: What?

PERRY: How will I explain this to my mother?
    I spent fifteen years getting her used
    To the idea I was gay.
    And now she'll jump to the conclusion
    I'm heterosexual after all.

LOU: Gays have children too.

PERRY: I know,
    But that's one step beyond her compre-
        hension.
    She's going to ask me all about you –
    What you do, how old you are –
    And then she'll say you're too old for me,
    And you must have trapped me into it;
    But still she'll demand
    I make an honest woman of you.
    Then she'll start asking about her grand-
        child,
    Whether it's a boy or girl,

	And knitting baby clothes.

LOU: Then don't tell her.

PERRY: How can I avoid it?
         You're lucky both your folks are dead,
         You don't have to tell them.

LOU: Don't say that –
         My mother died in excruciating pain
         Of cancer.

PERRY: I'm sorry. I forgot. I wasn't thinking.
         Hey, won't you need tests, or something?
         Some of those things are hereditary.
         And what about our blood groups?
         Maybe we won't be compatible.
         Won't I need tests too?

LOU: Relax. We'll do the tests together.
         We're in this for the long haul, right?

PERRY: Right.

LOU: Right.

BLACKOUT

Scene Seven

[A knock at PERRY and FLIP's front door. PERRY goes to it. It is BEV.]

BEV: Is Flip in?

PERRY: He's at Presto, doing the weekly shop.

BEV: I need to talk to you alone.

PERRY: Sure. Come in. Sit on the bed, please...

[She does so, very serious.]

PERRY: Coffee? *[Bev shakes her head.]* Gin?

BEV: *[A strained smile]* A bit early for me.

PERRY: Me too.

BEV: I'll come straight to the point.
                    Have you thought of testing?

PERRY: I talked it over with Lou.
                    Of course we'll have the usual tests
                    That would-be parents have.

BEV: What tests?

PERRY: Oh, I don't know.
            The usual tests, I suppose.
            Blood groups, things like that.

BEV: Are you being tested
            For this new disease?
            This gay plague that the papers talk about.
            H.I.V. or HTLV-Three –
            So confusing, names.
            There's a test – an ELISA test –
            You should take it.

PERRY: Me?

BEV: Just to be safe.

PERRY: You don't know what you're asking.
            What's the point of a test?
            It isn't even accurate;
            It tells you you're infected
            With something that hasn't got a cure –
            Or even a treatment?
            Besides we've been together, Flip and me,
            Since nineteen-eighty one.

BEV: And never been with anybody else?

PERRY: Well, sure, from time to time,
            Adventure here and there –
            But never with Americans.

How many cases have there been
Up here in the Midlands?
A handful.
There's less than a hundred deaths
In the whole country.

BEV: At the moment.

PERRY: And what if I did have it?
          Think of all the prejudice around.
          I could easily lose my job.
          If I'm going to have a death sentence
          I'd rather not know.
          Or I could go blind –
          I heard of someone,
          Kissed his lover on the ear
          On a flight to Texas
          And the ear fell off.

BEV: If it's going to happen,
          Then it's going to happen,
          Whether or not you know.
          Are you seriously saying
          You would risk infecting your best friend
          And possibly your baby?

PERRY: No, of course not.

BEV: Then you must do it.
          Take a test. Take two.

And Flip must go as well.

PERRY: Hey! Wait a minute!
I can't speak for him.

BEV: It's that, or nothing doing.

PERRY: How can you dictate what Lou decides?
Does she agree with you?

BEV: She always agrees with me.
She'd be a fool if she didn't.
Agreed? Agreed?

PERRY: You're pushing me to do this
Without discussing it with her?

BEV: I have to. Cos it's her baby.

PERRY: Our baby.

BEV: No, Perry. Her baby.
I'm the lawyer, trust me.
You can have all the dreams you want,
But in law the baby's Lou's.

PERRY: That can't be right.
I want to be a proper father.

BEV: The Children and Young Person's Act

Nineteen thirty two.
The biological father has no rights at all.
It will help if you are named
On the birth certificate,
To indicate an interest,
But are you getting married? No.
Are you going to live together?
Over my dead body.

PERRY: But we've agreed.

BEV: And if Lou changes her mind?
           What if you have a serious falling-out?
           What if she never wants to see you again?

PERRY: She won't be like that.

BEV: What if she dies?
           The child will go into care –
           Court of Protection.
           Will a judge want your baby
           Brought up by two queers?
           Or by a lesbian? No, don't look at me.
           You two are children,
           Babes in the Wood,
           Surrounded by thickets of regulation
           You don't even know,
           Let alone understand.

PERRY: You say, Talk to Flip –

And you haven't even talked to Lou
About all this.

BEV: I will. I will.
            I know I have to.
            But I don't want to be the villain,
            The one who's blamed for putting her off.
            If I must talk to Lou,
            You *must* talk to Flip.
            Deal?

PERRY: Deal.

BLACKOUT

Scene Eight

[BEV and PERRY. BEV has a petri dish in her hand. She is brisk and efficient to conceal her obvious distaste. She is still hoping it won't happen.]

BEV: You're sure you're negative?
            You give me your word?

PERRY: I told you. I tested twice.
            That's what we had to wait for.

BEV: And Flip as well?

PERRY: The same.

BEV: I'm sorry, but I'm nervous.

PERRY: *You're* nervous!

BEV: I've checked Lou's temperature,
            It's slightly up.
            She's going to ovulate
            In four days' time or so.
            Have you got everything you need?

PERRY: I don't need anything.

BEV: I thought you might need some porno-
            graphy.

288

That's what men do, don't they?
Masturbate to porn.
I got a copy of *Drummer*.

PERRY: *Drummer*? That's a leather magazine!

BEV: It seemed the most explicit and extreme.

PERRY: You think all gay men are into leather?
How little you know me!
I stopped using porn when I met Flip.
Who needs it when you have the real
    thing?

BEV: Why isn't he here, then?
If that's what floats your boat.

PERRY: He doesn't want anything to do with it.
The thought of heterosexual conception
Makes him physically nauseous.

BEV: That's absurd. All that happens is,
He holds you close and talks dirty
While you come into the petri dish.
Talking dirty is entirely homo,
You've done it a million times before

PERRY: How do you know?

BEV: I imagine.

PERRY: Not into a Petri dish.

BEV: The destination of your sperm
            Is no concern of yours.

PERRY: *[Protesting]* Pardon me?

BEV: Now, I'll be waiting with the turkey
              baster.
            When you've finished,
            Bring the petri dish to the door
            And I'll take it from you.
            Quick as you can, please.

PERRY: This clinical approach
            Really doesn't help
            To create an atmosphere.

BEV: I don't mean come as quick as you can;
            I mean, give me the dish after you've
              come
            As quickly as you can,
            So it's still warm
            While I insert it.

PERRY: You make it sound like a vet
            Inseminating a cow.

BEV: No... no!! It will be an act of love.
            Believe me, it will be an act of love.

[*Confidential*] Listen,
You know I think it's crazy.
If there was any way to stop it
Or to change her mind, I would.
But this is what Lou wants.
She wants it more than she wants me, I
    think.
So I must want what she wants,
Or I could lose her.
OK, I'll leave you to it.
I'll go and feed the dog.

[She exits, leaving PERRY sitting on the bed, looking around.]

PERRY: This is so weird.
A strange room –
A strange women's room,
Smelling of talc and Givenchy.

[He wanders round the room, curious. Looks at the ward-robe.]

Good god, girl! When did you buy that?!
Who's is it? Fake fur? Yuk!
Those shoulder pads must be Bev.

[Looks at books on the table.]

'You can negotiate anything'. That will be
Bev.

'Mrs Gaskell' – Lou.

[He pulls himself together.]

Come on, you're putting this off.
Should I take my clothes off,
Or just undo my flies?
Trousers round the ankles?
You haven't done that
Since that toilet in the Isle of Wight –
1974, that would have been.
I was nineteen, and lonely.
No… Clothes off, I think.

[He takes his clothes off, and sits on the bed, back to the audience. Takes the petri dish in hand.]

Gosh, it's cold in here.
Bev and Lou are hardy outdoor types.
Come here, you gorgeous petri dish.
[Parody sexy French accent]
Je t'aime, ma petite boîte de petri.
No. Concentrate…
Oh, Flip, I wish you were here.

[He starts wanking conscientiously as the lights fade to –]

BLACKOUT

Scene Nine

[PERRY and FLIP, both semi-naked on the bed. FLIP laughs.]

FLIP: You couldn't do it?

PERRY: It's no joke.
             Two hours I tried,
             Couldn't even get it up.
             And Bev didn't help,
             Coming in every twenty minutes –
             'Haven't you done it yet?'
             You'd think she didn't want it happen.
             I tried everything.
             I touched myself up all over,
             I thought of you doing it to me.
             I thought of Nick Kamen doing it to me.
             Limp as a wilted lettuce.

FLIP: You poor baby. I'll soon put you right.

[Gently takes him and kisses him. He looks down at PERRY.]

FLIP: See? Nothing wrong with you.

[He starts to get horny with PERRY.]

PERRY: No, we shouldn't.
             I've promised to go back to Lou

	To try again later. I ought to save myself.
FLIP:	'Save yourself!' You sound like a girl from a sixties beach movie. Annette Funicello or Sandra Dee. Semen isn't finite, you know, You're not using up your allowance. Come here, Sandra...
PERRY:	Won't you come to Lou's with me Next time? Please...
FLIP:	It's more likely to make me soft Than to make you hard.
PERRY:	You don't have to be hard Just make me hard.
FLIP:	No! I couldn't sit there, in their house, Doing that. I took the test for you – twice. What more do you want?
PERRY:	You were negative.
FLIP:	*[Long pause.]* Actually – The second time, I was positive. The first time, it was negative,

I didn't tell you about the second.

PERRY: How could you do that?
         This changes everything,
         We can't go through with it.

FLIP: That's such a shame. But you are right.

PERRY: Are you sure you have the virus?

FLIP: Would I lie about a thing like that?

PERRY: Show me the result.

FLIP: I threw it away.

PERRY: Have another test.

FLIP: No. Two is quite enough.

PERRY: I can't believe it.
         You wouldn't do this to me.

FLIP: To you? I'm the one
         Who's dealing with a death sentence.

PERRY: It's not just you, it's me and Lou.

FLIP: Sometimes I think you love her more
             than me.

PERRY: Of course I don't.
            I really wanted that baby.

FLIP: We could just stop having sex,
            Never have sex ever again.
            Then you could have your precious baby.

PERRY: Yes... we could do that...

FILP: Are you serious?
            [Getting up] OK, I'm leaving.

PERRY: What are you talking about?

FLIP: If you want that baby so much,
            And a leper's in your way,
            The leper will go roam the world.
            Unclean! Unclean!

PERRY: Don't be so absurd.

FLIP: Nothing absurd about it.
            Wait three months, have another test.
            If you're clear, then you and Lou can do it.
            I won't be in your way.

PERRY: I don't know. I love you.
            I can't imagine life without you.
            I want you – I want the baby –
            I can't think straight.

FLIP: Or we could keep things exactly as they
                   are.

[Goes to put his arms round PERRY.]

PERRY: *[Shouts]* Get off of me!

                   BLACKOUT

Scene Ten

[LOU and BEV's flat. LOU is lying on the bed, under the duvet. BEV comes in, turkey baster and petri dish in hand.]

LOU: Did it work?

BEV: Well, there's something in the dish,
                   And I don't think it's egg white.

LOU: Third time lucky.

BEV: Part one accomplished.
                   Now for part two.

[BEV is leaning over LOU. The turkey baster and the Petri dish to hand. She looks at an alarm clock. She kisses LOU very tenderly. Prolongs it. LOU breaks off.]

LOU: Shouldn't we get on with it?
                   How long will that sperm survive?

BEV: We have ages. Come here.

[Kisses her again. A thought.]

BEV: I have to check if Perry's okay.
                   I just rushed in here and left him.

LOU: And with good reason.

BEV: Don't worry, I know what I am doing.
                I'll tell him to make himself some tea
                And have some biscuits,
                Like the blood donors do.

[Exits. LOU looks in the petri dish dubiously. Sniffs it. BEV comes back.]

BEV: He's fine. He wants to stay
                And see how it worked out.

LOU: We'd better get a move on then –
                Come here.

Aria

BEV: *[Holding her]* Don't be so cold,
                This is really special.
                I feel so close to you now.
                This is the most intimate thing
                That we have ever done.
                Here, let me spread you like a flower…
                I can feel you opening
                Underneath my hand.

[LOU arches her back to accommodate BEV.]

                I can never say how much I love you.
                You are my heart, my life, my everything.
                I never feel alive without you,

My pulse beats to the beat of your heart,
I feel it now in my blood,
My heart answers.
When I am away, my focus is all you.
I wonder what you're doing.
Where you are, what you're thinking,
Who you're with, how you're feeling.

[She has been working LOU up with her fingers.]

LOU: We must do the business –

BEV: I love it when you're wet,
              And now I feel you dripping
              Underneath my fingers.
              Come for me, my Lou, my love.
              I want to feel you coming,
              Your contractions round my hand,
              So soft, yet strong.

LOU: Please – Perry's –

BEV: Soon it will come, will come,
              The spirit that will give you
              Your blessed golden child.

* * *

[She takes the turkey baster and inserts it.]

BEV: Can you feel that?

LOU: Yes, oh yes.

BEV: I'm stroking your clit, darling.
                I love your clit so much,
                It leaps to my touch.

LOU: No – yes –
                Give me the sperm…

BEV: I'm going to –
                Yes –

LOU: Yes. I am ready.
                My walls are red with blood,
                And aching for it…
                Oh – oh – oh –

[She comes. Lies back exhausted. The alarm clock goes off. LOU looks at it.]

LOU: What the – ? What was that?

BEV: It's time, darling. The time is now.

[Smiles with satisfaction. BEV squeezes the turkey baster. LOU quivers.]

FADE TO BLACKOUT

Scene Eleven

[BEV and LOU's flat. PERRY rings. BEV makes him stand in the door.]

BEV: Oh Perry, I'm so sorry.
          I heard about Flip.

PERRY: How did you know?

BEV: He told me.

PERRY: He told you, but not me?

BEV: He was concerned about Lou.
          He thought she should know
          Straight away.

PERRY: And I shouldn't? This makes no sense.

BEV: He wanted me to break it to her gently.

PERRY: Can I see her?

BEV: She doesn't want to see you.
          As far as she's concerned,
          You've trashed her dream,
          Your sperm has poisoned her.

PERRY: Let her tell me that herself.

BEV: No way. She's too fragile.
            Besides, she's asleep.

PERRY: When can I see her?

BEV: I'll let you know.

PERRY: I don't trust you.
            There's something going on.
            [Calls] Lou! Lou!

BEV: You'd better go.

PERRY: Lou!

BEV: I'll set the dog on you.

PERRY: You wouldn't.

BEV: Sheba! Sheba! *[An answering bark off-
            stage.]*

PERRY: *[Going]* I'll be back. *[Gets increasingly
            agitated.]*

BEV: Yeah! You and Arnold Schwarzenegger.

PERRY: This is kidnapping.

BEV: You can't kidnap your own wife.

PERRY: And you can't hold her prisoner.

BLACKOUT

Scene Twelve

[The park again. LOU and PERRY, with a pram.]

LOU: Isn't she beautiful?

PERRY: Yes she is. Takes after me.

LOU: Shut up!

PERRY: It was all lies, of course.
That shit Flip fed you
About girl and boy babies.

LOU: It wasn't just him.
I heard it elsewhere too,
Kind of urban myth.

PERRY: No, it was Flip.
He was so full of shit.
Nothing but lies, all of it.
He never had H.I.V., you know.

LOU: How did you find out?

PERRY: It never really added up.
Why didn't he tell me straight away?
It was only when we started to get serious –
You, me and the turkey baster.

305

LOU: He must have really hated the idea of that
            baby.

PERRY: And he never behaved like he had the
            virus –
            Never seemed upset enough.

LOU: You knew him too well.

PERRY: He was just a bad actor.
            I threatened to get on to the Mortimer,
            Tell them he was my partner,
            And refusing to tell me his result.

LOU: They never would have given it to you.

PERRY: I know that.
            But Flip could be remarkably naïve.
            He spilled the beans.

LOU: And Bev went with it.
            She knew all along.
            Tried to frighten us off.

PERRY: She never seemed too worried
            I might have given you H.I.V.

LOU: And all the lovey-dovey stuff
            When she had the turkey baster
            Was just to let the sperm cool down

So it was useless.
Though it was horny as hell.
Thank you for rescuing me.
She was using the dog
To keep me trapped in that flat.
I was terrified.

PERRY: That was one of the scariest moments
         Of my life, when Sheba went for me.
         Just as well I thought to buy
         Some long cowhide gloves,
         A shield against a vicious dog.

LOU: I thought you'd choke that poor Alsatian.

PERRY: Poor? That dog would have had my hand
         off.

LOU: Because she was trained that way.

PERRY: It's over now.

LOU: And here we are.
         The three of us.

Duet

LOU: Here with our girl,
         Our shot at the future,
         Our hostage to the world.

Our flesh, our love,
Our hope, our DNA.

Perry: It sails through us,
        Out of us,
        It sails down the river of time
        Towards eternity.

BOTH: We are the vehicle,
        The vehicle of life,
        And all our petty self
        Is unimportant,
        In face of such a charge.

[Into the pram, a lullaby:]

LOU: You lie so still and fast asleep.

PERRY: I dare not breathe, my watch to keep.

BOTH: Everything so new and clean,
        Sweetest child there's ever been.

LOU: Think I see a lovely view,
        A sunlit road ahead,
        All laid out for you.

PERRY: So I wish you a gentle breeze.
        You'll gently rock on clear blue seas.

BOTH: And every day
               We'll keep you warm, we'll keep you dry,
               Every day.
               We'll guard you with a careful eye,
               You'll never want for anything.
               We'll let you live in a perpetual spring.
               We'll keep you safe, we'll watch you grow,
               You'll make us feel so proud, we know.
               And if you cry, as cry you may,
               Then we will kiss your tears away.
               We wish you health, we wish you hope,
               And lucky stars in your horoscope.
               We wish you friends so strong and true;
               We hope they're always there for you.
               So sleep your sleep
               And dream your dreams;
               We're watching over you,
               So you can be
               Who you can be.

PERRY: That'll be enough for me,
               Quite enough for me.

LOU: Enough to please me too.

Quartet

[The voices of BEV and FLIP come in, either onstage or off in counterpoint.]

BEV: It's better far this way,
                    There's a new life to be had.

FLIP: I really couldn't stay,
                    A kid would drive me mad.

BOTH: We each have our own life to lead.

BEV: I have a career
                    Where I need to succeed.

FLIP: Have a joint, have a beer,
                    Have some coke, have some speed.

BEV: My whole life a perpetual marathon,
                    I'm on my marks at the starting blocks
                    Now the kid has gone.
                    There's nowhere I'm as happy as in court,
                    Proving I should be a silk – in short,
                    In the Crown Court, when the judge has
                        slumbered,
                    I'm often out-gunned, oft outnumbered;
                    Yet as long as I'm unencumbered,
                    Always I'll prevail
                    Over any male.

Who cares if I go to an empty flat?
My independence is where it's at.
Tell me, what the hell is wrong with that?
It's my life to do what I want to do;
And what the fuck is that to any of you?
What? What?

FLIP: Look at me, I'm so young, yes! Young and
                    cute.
                  All the horny guys come in hot pursuit,
                  And there's nothing like feeling you're
                    admired
                  If your body's on fire to be desired.
                  My mother wished I'd been aborted;
                  Dad's ambitions always thwarted,
                  But now by the hottest hunks I'm courted –
                  I feed on their affection,
                  Feeling their erection.
                  Who cares if there's disease around?
                  I'll go where lights of love are found –
                  Throw me a lifeline before I'm drowned.
                  Please... Please...

ALL: Who can identify mistakes?
                  Who knows if they do right?
                  The Fates can tell us, but they're not
                    replying.
                  And life itself flows on,
                  To disappear from sight,
                  Leaving us, the living and the dying.

Coda

*[FLIP and BEV fade away, leaving LOU and PERRY with
the pram.]*

LOU:	You know, people walking past Would take us for a married couple. *[Pause.]* A young heterosexual married couple.
PERRY:	Young-ish
LOU:	OK, young-ish… *[Pause.]*
PERRY:	Of course we could get married –
LOU:	*[Dubious]* We could –
PERRY:	I'm free, as Mr Humphries says. *[He quotes, shrill:]* I'm FREEE!
LOU:	And I'm – I'm Bev-less; No wife, no dog…
PERRY:	No home… *[Pause.]*
PERRY:	In many ways it would make life easier, Getting married.
LOU:	After what we've been through,

Anything would be easier.

PERRY: I am a little in love with you, you know.

LOU: Oh, please, don't spoil it.
Your heterosexuality
Is like your appendix,
A vestigial organ
Which does nothing but grumble.

PERRY: But we could —

LOU: No! A thousand times no!
Where's your self-respect?

PERRY: I was thinking of the baby;
It would be easier.

LOU: Easier for her to know
Her parents were both liars?
There's more to life than easiness.
Let's stick to sharing the baby,
That's quite enough to do.

BOTH: Share the baby,
Enjoy our little girl,
Our shot at the future —
That's quite enough to do.

FADE TO BLACKOUT

A Gay Century: 15

1988: Eric Lives With Martin and Jenny

A Powerpoint Presentation

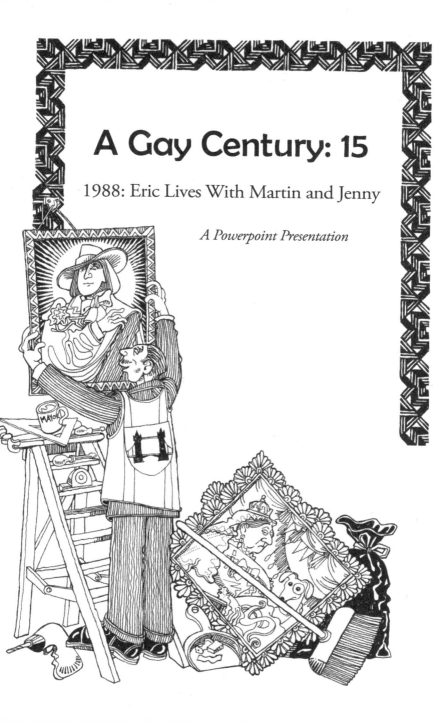

Above: *The book in the Inner London Education Authority library which led indirectly to the introduction of Section 28*
Below: *Dame Jill Knight*

Introduction

*J*enny Lives with Eric and Martin was a Danish children's
book designed to introduce very young children to the
idea that some young people grow up with two Daddies or
two Mummies. It was published in Denmark in 1981, and
translated into English in 1983. There was a solitary copy
of this English version in an Inner London Education
Authority's Teacher Centre, as a resource for teachers. It
was never made generally available in schools.

However, once the press had got hold of this fact, it
became a story about how Loony Left councils were
forcing children to 'become gay' all over London. So bad
was the coverage that the school and the I.L.E.A. made
formal complaints to the Press Council about the lies in
the *Daily Mail* and the like. The Press Council, being con-
stituted by the Press itself, did nothing. The book was con-
demned by the Secretary of State for Education, Kenneth
Baker, who also, at the height of the A.I.D.S. pandemic,
forbad education about safer sex in schools.

One of the foremost campaigners against 'gay propaganda' in schools was Dame Jill Knight, ennobled in 1985.
She and David Wilshire introduced Clause 14, later to
become Section 28, as an amendment to the Local Government Act 1988. This forbade councils to 'promote
homosexuality' as a 'pretended family relationship'. She
claimed in parliament that children under two had access
to lesbian and gay books in the London Borough of

317

Lambeth. The claim has never been substantiated, but if true, it would have demonstrated a remarkable level of literacy south of the river.

But what of the characters themselves, and their story? *Jenny Lives with Eric and Martin* is a sweet, not to say saccharine, tale of a five-year-old in a run-of-the-mill household taking part in activities like having breakfast with the dads in bed, doing the washing, mending a bike, planting potatoes. Jenny is also introduced to the idea that some people don't like homosexuals, and also that gay dads sometimes quarrel [over the potatoes]. It is all very gentle and positive – but is it the true story?

Jenny is Martin's daughter, but here in this alternative take, his lover Eric tells a different story: that of a demanding little girl who was foisted on them, whom Eric resents passionately. She has disrupted their fun gay life in Copenhagen, and things can never be the same again – or can they?

This scenario – monologue almost – was originally intended as a pendant to the cycle of *The Gay Century* proper, because some of its themes are encompassed in the character of Flip in the previous *1986: A Shot at the Future*. It is included here in the hope that it might one day be a stand-alone concert aria of the kind written by Haydn and Mozart in the 18th century, accompanied by a slide show. Its drama would enliven a recital considerably.

To make sense, this piece needs the pictures in the order and at the place where they occur in the text. The pictures are taken from the original book published by Gay Men's Press in this country in 1984, photographs by Andres

Hansen. Neither the original Danish publisher Fremåd nor GMP are in business any longer; efforts by the GMP directors to contact either the author or the photographer have been unsuccessful. If either cares to contact us, we will be happy to reach an accommodation.

CAST

ERIC: Counter-tenor
A gay man in his early 30s. Smart casual – check shirt, jeans, wispy moustache.

DAME JILL KNIGHT: Mezzo-Soprano
A formidable Conservative MP, perm like a helmet, twinset and pearls, around 60.

SPEAKER OF THE HOUSE OF COMMONS: Voice Off, spoken.

SETTING

Bare stage with one wooden chair; and a screen on which to project a slide show. ERIC will talk directly to the audience, DAME JILL in a spotlight at the rear of the stage will grandstand as if addressing a large meeting.

The slides and the order in which they appear is so important that I have introduced them into the text where they are referred to.

INSTRUMENTS

Piano solo

ERIC LIVES WITH MARTIN AND JENNY

[Bare stage]

VOICE OFF: *[spoken]* The Honourable Member for Birmingham Edgbaston.

DAME JILL: *[Over a hubbub of cheers and boos:]*
Thank you, Mister Speaker.
Many parents are concerned
About the books in schools;
So-called sex education books,
Which may corrupt our children.
There is shocking evidence in abundance
That children are being encouraged
To be gay and lesbian,
Some as young as five years old.
This is paid for out of the rates,
Against the wishes of the parents.

There is a book called *The Milkman's on his Way*.
I will not shock the House by quoting from it.
It shows intercourse in sordid detail
Between an adolescent boy
And his adult male lover.

Haringey Council made a video,

How to become a lesbian in thirty five
  minutes.
It was shown to mentally handicapped
  girls.

There has also been a deal of protest
About *Jenny Lives with Eric and Martin.*
It shows a little girl of six,
In bed with her father and his male lover,
Both of whom are naked.

They all live happily together.
It is terrifying to me
That local councils have been promoting
That kind of stuff.

This is a pile of filth
All paid for by the rates.

[Spotlight fades. Lights more generally on ERIC.]

ERIC: There I am on the right in the photo,
Martin on the left with the skinny arms.
I hate that photo.
It makes me look a porker
With that double chin.

You can tell we're Danish –
We eat crispbread in bed,
With reckless disregard
For the viciousness of crumbs.
And Jenny wants some jam.
She's always wanting something.
She's a pain in the butt.
I hate that girl,
It's all her fault
We're in this mess now.

I was an average young gay man
In Copenhagen,
Cruising round the bars,
The Intime, and the Centralhjornet
The Cozy Bar and the Masken.

I didn't have a moustache in those days
I was young and clean-cut,

323

And everyone wanted a piece of me –
I never went home alone.

Then I met Martin,
Who looked deep in my eyes
And talked of love.

He was so squeaky clean and certain;
He offered calm where I had known
Only adrenalin and inconstancy.

At first he didn't tell me he was married,
To a woman called Karen.
But when I found out, that was cool.

I was content to be the other man
In a triangle with a bisexual;
That was very hip, that was Danish.
It left me time to pick up other men
And go to backrooms.

I loved the bushes in the Orstedsparken,
The playroom and the darkroom
At the SLM.
The voices whispering dirty in your ear,
The smell of sweat and cum and baby oil.
Hard, hard bodies you could only feel,
    not see –
Then back to Martin.

But Karen threw a spanner in the works,
The bitch, by spawning.

I think she came off the pill
Without telling him,
To get herself pregnant.
It's what some women do
To get what they want.

That isn't Karen in the picture,
She's played by some model.
By the time we took the pictures for the
   book,
The real Karen had done a bunk.

I couldn't meet with Martin any more,
Not the way I had before.
He had to babysit,
He had to go to clinics,
He had to look for kindergartens;
Always something
For the stupid brat.

Still I saw him, of course,
Cos no-one gave him blow jobs like I did.
He wasn't going to give up fun com-
   pletely
For the sake of any child.

We jogged along…
I accommodated…

I have always been accommodating,

In bed and out of it.

But Karen hadn't wrecked my life
  enough,
She had to want a divorce –
And no, she didn't want the wretched girl.

Jenny…
Did I say her name was Jenny?
Cutsie-wootsie Jenny –
It makes me sick!

Why Karen couldn't take the girl
Is quite beyond me.
That's what women do, isn't it?
Bring up children,
Juggle with a home and a career,
And everyone admires how they cope.

But no, Karen had to get a job
Designing Lego bricks,
And move to Billund.

She took him to the cleaners
In the settlement:
The house and everything,
Which she sold.
Selfishly she wouldn't take the girl;
Left Martin holding the baby,
Literally.

He asked if he could move in –
He had no place of his own.
And me, I'm soft as shit, so I said yes.
That was fine for a year or two.
I still got out to the lake and the forest
At Charlottenlund,
Where there's a lot of action;
The sauna at the Copenhagen Gay
    Centre.

I have a high sex drive,
I can't help it.
So what?

But Martin starts to worry;
We are two gay parents,
We have to set an example.
And if we are to be an example,

We must be twice as good,
As well-behaved, as patient,
As any straights.

I am not a gay parent…
I did not choose this…
Did Martin ask me?
Did Karen ask me?
No they did not!

[ERIC brings a washing line across the stage, sets it up. He then gets a basket of clean washing – Jenny's little clothes – and starts to peg them out.]

You see? How I'm reduced
To being a good little housewife?
You would not believe
How many clothes that girl gets through.

Cack in her knickers,
Jam down her tank top,
Rolling in the dirt –
Unbelievable!

Then along comes Martin's friend,
Suzanne Bosche.
'Let me write a book about you,'
She says.
'We'll show the world
How gay men can be as normal
As everybody else.'

I don't want to be normal!

I did not come out,
I did not struggle for my liberation,
So I could be like all the rest.

Whatever else they say,
Liberation is about sex.
The more sex you can have,
The more liberated you are.

But Suzanne persuaded Martin,
And we posed for stupid pictures...

Jenny loved to pose for pictures.
Proper little diva, a real madam,
Always the centre of attention.

When me and Martin wanted sex in the
    morning –
And I love sex in the morning –

She was always pushing in.

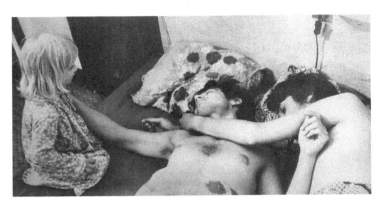

Here we are, another photo,
Waking up, getting excited –
And it's 'Make my breakfast, Daddy' –
'Come and play with me, Daddy' –
No thought for anybody else.

You can't see it in the picture,
But underneath that duvet
I have a massive erection.

But Susanne's story
Was so boring and bourgeois:
Going to the launderette,
Mowing the lawn,
Tending the garden.

She was obsessed by potatoes,
Growing them, digging them up,

Eating them – 'Mmmm!' *[He makes a
    face.]*
She even had us
Giving potatoes as presents –
Dull, dull, dull, dull, dull!

The most exciting thing I ever did
Was mend a puncture in a tyre
On my bicycle.

See? She can't even let us cook a meal
Without she wants to join in –
And let me tell you, her cooking's shit!
Martin's trying to make
Spaghetti Bolognese,
And what does she put in it?
Sugar sprinkles!

Talking of presents,
When it was my birthday,
All I wanted was to get wrecked:
A bit of spliff, a bottle of good wine.
But no, we had to have
Jellies, fairy cakes and candles,
Cocoa and fizzy drinks,
Because she was there –
Not even a bottle of Carlsberg!

It's not Jenny's birthday,
It's mine for Christ sake!
And if I want to get wrecked,
I bloody well will.

Of course we rowed about it,
Martin and me.
But thanks to Jenny
We couldn't even row properly.
From the pictures
You'd think I was asking,

'One lump or two'.
And of course the little limpet
Had to get in on it as well.
Look at her in the middle –
Poisonous poppet!

[Pause. He looks at the picture.]

Shame, cos Martin has a really nice arse,
Not that I've had it for months.

The trouble with that Suzanne Bosche
Who wrote our book,
Everything has to be sweetness and light;
Even her queerbashers are middle class.
Real gays get skinheads
With swastikas and tattoos,

Bricks through the windows,
DMs in the guts.
That would show young Jenny
What it's all about.

But no, we get Miss Judi Dench,
Whose worst insult is 'Oh, you gays!
What on earth do you think you're
    playing at?
Why don't you stay at home
So the rest of us don't have to see you?'
Obviously we're terrified – NOT!
Look at me! I'm bloody smiling!

Whoever met a queerbasher
Old enough to be their mother?

[He has finished putting out the washing. He looks at it, then comes to a decision and tears the washing off the line.]

To hell with it, I've had enough.
I want a normal life.
A normal gay life,
With a high disposable income
To spend on clothes,
And going to clubs,
And fashionable restaurants,
A gym membership
And sex toys,
A small mews house that's
A neglected gem,
Which I can restore myself,
In an area I will help to gentrify.

I want to get bladdered on a Friday,
Dance to six A.M.,
Chill out in some calm café,
Where drugs may be available,
Through a long lazy afternoon,
With Carly Simon and Brian Eno.

We were happy as we were,
Martin and me.
We had a life of our own,
Before that wretched Jenny
Came to live with us.

[A thought, and a decision.]

> I have the answer!
> If Jenny could come to live,
> Then Jenny can go.
> Jenny can go – Now!
> To hell with sentiment!
> Who is she to come into my life
> Uninvited,
> Take it over, turn me into
> Someone I am not?
> I have to destroy her,
> This atrocious infant,
> To save myself.

[He calls offstage:]

> Jenny! Where are you, darling?
> Uncle Eric's got a game for you.

[He unties the washing line, and coils it in his hand. He exits. The following lines are delivered offstage –]

> Would you like a little game?
> A little bondage game?
> Perhaps a little mild asphyxiation…

[The music rises to a climax as ERIC strangles JENNY in the washing line. The music suggests an intense struggle, with JENNY gradually getting weaker, and the struggle dying

away. ERIC staggers back onto the stage with a large – very large – doll caught round the neck in the washing line. This can be the one used in 'A Shot at the Future'. He raises it above his head, suspended in the rope. Triumphant:]

LIBERATION!

BLACKOUT

A Gay Century: 16

1999: Skin Deep

A song of hope

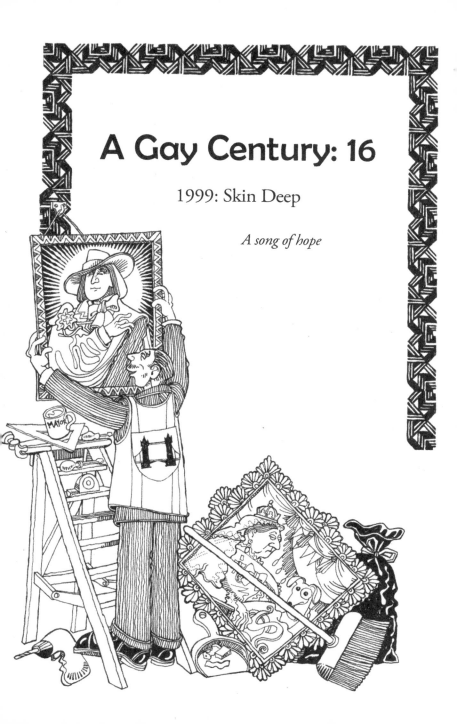

Above: *April 1999: Outside the Admiral Duncan immediately after the bombing*
Below: *There is an annual ceremony of remembrance for the Admiral Duncan bombing*

Introduction

When I first had the idea of the opera-per-decade structure of *A Gay Century*, my first thought was that the emotional climax had to be the Admiral Duncan bombings of 1999. This was our heart of darkness, the moment that reminded us of the fragile nature of our gains and the shaky foundations of our newly-acquired confidence. It would need to dive deep into the blackness, in order to emerge stronger for the experience.

At that stage, in late 2019, I had the bones of the plot and the characters which would conform to Robert's and my constraints of seven performers in total: three main actors and an all-purpose extra. To enhance the sense of community it also needed an off-stage chorus.

The bombing of the Admiral Duncan on the eve of the Spring Bank Holiday in 1999 sent shock waves through the London – indeed the UK – LGBT community like no other event. There had been arrests, police raids, abuse and violence before, but this was different. Different in scale and approach. Three people killed, 74 injured. The injuries, caused by 1500 four-inch nails, were devastating. People lost arms, legs, eyes. The so-called cosmetic injuries – and cosmetic injuries are never only cosmetic, because they puncture the very sense of self – caused supreme anguish beyond the physical pain. While those who were present but escaped physical injury still report, twenty years later, flashbacks and nightmares.

Different too was the whole approach of bomber David Copeland. The Admiral Duncan bombing was the third such, following one in Brixton Market [Afro-Caribbean community – 48 injured] and Brick Lane [Bangladeshi community – 13 injured]. As never before, we felt physically connected to other minorities and their struggles; I think it is fair to say that we would not have the brown and black bands on the modern Pride flag representing people of colour, had it not been for the Copeland bombings.

The whole idea of planting bombs in gathering and meeting places in this way has become more common in the 21st century, with tactics imported from on the one hand the Middle East conflicts and from the Alt-Right in America on the other. It has hardened us. We accept the intrusive armed police, the crash barriers on Waterloo Bridge. London in 2005, Manchester in 2017: the tolls were greater, but somehow the concept of defence in a war of terror was now part of our psyche, in a way that it wasn't in 1999, unless you were from Northern Ireland. There were IRA activities in the UK too, of course, but in a strange way, at least to the LGBT population, they had seemed distant, none of our business.

Skin Deep focuses on three survivors of the bombing, and the ways in which they cope with it. One is terribly injured, and plunges into depression and despair. Another is filled with guilt because she wasn't in the pub when her friend was, and she should have been. The third, Queenie, is loosely based on the barman, later manager, of the *Admiral Duncan*, David Morley, affectionately known as Sinders. Morley showed astonishing heroism in helping during the bombing, and the patience of a saint supporting victims afterwards. This was at great personal cost, suppressing his own trauma. Having survived, he was himself killed by some mindless young thugs five years later. But I emphasis this is not documentary, this is a work of fiction. It is subtitled *A Song of Hope*.

All my work is about redemption and the possibility of change in some form or another. It was particularly important in *Skin Deep*, which is the keystone to the whole edifice which is *The Gay Century*. It is the penultimate opera, but *2001: Two into One* is more of an epilogue, to mirror the prologue in *1900: Two Queens*.

Skin Deep had to delve into the deepest recesses of despair; what, I asked, could bring somebody – Frankie – back to the land of the living having lost his looks, his job, his health, his lover? The knife is twisted by losing his place in a community obsessed with youth and beauty. At one point he tries to go back to a disco he used to frequent, only to have the security staff tell him to piss off because the sight of him will upset the other customers. Lest this seem too harsh and melodramatic, I can only report that I've seen it happen to a friend of mine with spastic cerebral palsy at a well-known London club. In fairness, there were also places where he was welcomed.

Where then the hope? Perhaps the most touching story I came across about the aftermath was of a group of Bangladeshi lads who turned up at the *Admiral Duncan* a week after the bombing, with a condolence card. They had been on their way to the East London Mosque when the Brick Lane bomb exploded. They'd been through a similar ordeal, they knew what it was like. Not, you might think, the group of people most immediately likely to respond in this way, but simple humanity and solidarity won through.

So too did the memory of Sinders and his example. Every year there are commemorations of the bombing in an open-air ceremony led by Fr Simon, the delightful rector of St Anne's Soho, the church over the road from the pub. It's a sad occasion, but also a coming together in solidarity where the story of Sinders, his generous life and his bravery, lives again. This year was the twentieth anniversary of the bombing, but for many it is as immediate as it was on April 30th, 1999.

In this resilience, and its enduring memory, is a symbol perhaps of the whole story of the 20th century: the gay century.

Peter Scott-Presland
21 March 2021

CAST

FRANKIE BRAY: Tenor
20s, a pub regular, not what you'd think of as politically active or aware. Very good looking. In a relationship, but still a good-time guy.

QUEENIE: Bass
30s, a bar manager, a mother hen type – camp and quite fearless.

JODIE: Soprano
Frankie's best friend and work colleague, 20s, straight

PLUS: Multiple parts for one actor of either gender or none.

MUSIC NOTES

There is a disco/pub sound track [Standard, not to be written] which fades in and fades out, in order to go into and out of the *Admiral Duncan*. The onstage music plays over that in the first scene when QUEENIE is serving – it should be a bit discordant, a bit of an effort.

There is an offstage choir [soundtrack] for the ending.

SETTING

A bare stage, but a bed which is brought forward for certain hospital scenes. Other changes achieved by lighting.

INSTRUMENTS

Harp, flute, saxophone/s [doubled]

SKIN DEEP

Scene One

[Bare stage. FRANKIE, QUEENIE and JODIE in separate spotlights. FRANKIE and JODIE in barista aprons.]

FRANKIE: It was a bloody awful day at work –

JODIE: A bloody awful day.
I hate being a barista –

FRANKIE: I love being a barista.
I love the skill of a manual espresso.

JODIE: Having to be nice all the time –

FRANKIE: Grinding all the beans,
But not too much or they go sour.

JODIE: Laugh at all the stupid jokes
Of men who think they're funny.

FRANKIE: Espresso's temperamental,
Only gives its best
If you treat it gently.

JODIE: Little big shots,
Think they're something.

FRANKIE: A bit like a pick-up,
             Come to think of it.

JODIE: But at least I get time off
             To go to auditions.

FRANKIE: Still, it was an awful day –

JODIE: Awful day –

FRANKIE: The machine broke down…

JODIE: I was goosed…

FRANKIE: Goosed?!

JODIE: Yes, goosed!

FRANKIE: How quaint!
             Nobody's been goosed since
             Nineteen-eighty two.

JODIE: It wasn't funny.

FRANKIE: Sorry.

JODIE: My feet were killing me –

FRANKIE: The air-con on the blink –

JODIE: I'd been on my feet –

FRANKIE: I'd been on my feet –

BOTH: Since seven-thirty.

[They look at each other, nod, and take off their aprons.]

BOTH: Let's go to Soho.

JODIE: Do you want to call Andrew?

FRANKIE: Maybe later,
              If I feel like clubbing.
              What about Ollie?

JODIE: We had a bit of a barney.
              Let him stew.
              This one is for us.

BOTH: Let's go to Soho!

[The pub disco soundtrack fades in. QUEENIE comes to life, polishing a glass.]

QUEENIE: We're expecting a rush in Soho.
              It's quiet now, but in an hour or two
              It will be heaving.

[To an unseen customer:]
Is that your bag?
Well, keep it with you, doll.
I thought it was a bomb.
No, seriously.
Haven't you seen the posters?
We have to keep a look-out
Since Brick Lane.

[To the audience:]
Dizzy gym queen!

It's drinking all that Red Bull,
Rots the brain.

Mind you… I wouldn't say no,
Wouldn't kick him out of bed.
Lovely eyes –
Even if there's nothing much behind
  them.

[To himself:] What are you like?
Stop it. You have work to do.

*[Puts down the glass cloth, moves to another part of the stage,
behind the bar.]*

What will you have, doll?
Pint of IPA?
Just finished work, have we?

Going on anywhere later?
I reckon G-A-Y will be packed tonight –
Bank holiday weekend…

[He hands over the pint.]

There, get that down you.
You've earned it, I'm sure.
That'll be two pound twenty, please.

[QUEENIE freezes, lights down on that area. Disco soundtrack fades. Lights up on the forestage, which is the street outside the pub. JODIE and FRANKIE re-enter, stand near the pub entrance.]

JODIE: No, I'll get them. It's my round.

FRANKIE: Are you sure?

JODIE: You got them in the Joiner's Arms, remember?

FRANKIE: When was that?

JODIE: Karaoke night. You sang It's Raining Men, Almost cleared the pub.

FRANKIE: My mind's a sieve.
            [He remembers something:]
            No, you're wrong.

You got them at the Vauxhall.
That was Sunday,
The Sunday Social.

JODIE: I don't remember.

FRANKIE: *[Mock despair, to the audience:]* What is
            she like?

            [To JODIE:] What are you having?

JODIE: A pint of foaming meths!
            'Gonna wash that Starbucks out of my
                throat'...
            Amstel, please.

FRANKIE: Good idea. Me too.

JODIE: I'll stay out here and have a fag.

FRANKIE: You can smoke inside you know.
            Nanny hasn't made it *yet* a crime.

JODIE: It's so hot in there,
            And though I love a smoke,
            I can't stand the smell of other people's.

FRANKIE: OK, OK. I won't be long.
            Don't go wandering off.
            Excuse me. Excuse me.

[FRANKIE *mimes making his way through a crowded doorway. Lighting lowers – some filters. Disco music swells again. It becomes louder and louder. As it does, all the lights slowly fade to* BLACKOUT. *An almighty explosion, followed by absolute silence. The lights come up abruptly on* JODIE. *There is smoke billowing everywhere, and debris.*]

Aria

JODIE: It was weird, the silence,
        But that's what I remember.
        For a few seconds,
        Nothing but silence:
        Too shocked to move,
        To speak.
        I could hear a bird
        High over St Anne's churchyard,
        And my own feet
        Crunching on broken glass.

[*She comes to, and runs towards the door.*]

        Frankie! Frankie!

[*To the audience:*]

        People limping out
        Covered in blood…
        I saw a boy with nails
        Sticking in his face.

One boy got a nail in his eye...
Suddenly there was noise again,
Screaming.
Frankie! Frankie!

[QUEENIE carries FRANKIE out, like a pieta, and lays him down on the ground. FRANKIE's face is unrecognisable with blood, and his legs are at an awkward angle. QUEENIE too is covered in blood. His clothes are hanging off and he has a huge gash in his arm. FRANKIE is unconscious.]

JODIE: Careful where you put him.
            Mind the glass! There's glass everywhere.

QUEENIE: Mind the glass? After that?

[Puts ear to FRANKIE's chest. To JODIE:]

            He's still breathing.
            Well, what are you standing there for,
            You dozy cow?

JODIE: Ambulance... get an ambulance...

[She wanders vaguely off. QUEENIE draws her back.]

QUEENIE: Pull yourself together.
            There's help on the way,
            And more to get out
            From inside.

[He makes to go back in.]

JODIE: How many are there hurt?

QUEENIE: How the fuck should I know?
            I saw one girl with her leg took off,
            Not much more than twenty.
            I got to go and help,
            Get them out.
            They need me in there,
            They're my people.

JODIE: Yes, of course.

*[QUEENIE disappears through the smoke. JODIE holds
FRANKIE's hand. FRANKIE groans and stirs.]*

JODIE: *[To audience:]*
            They told us afterwards
            There were fifteen hundred nails in that
                bomb.
            There were eighty two in Frankie.

FRANKIE: What's going on? I can't see.

JODIE: Shhh. Quiet. Lie still.

FRANKIE: I can't feel anything.

JODIE: It's the shock.

FRANKIE: I can't feel my legs.

JODIE: The medics will be here soon,
                They're on the way.

[Woman's voice offstage, drunk and slurred.]

WOMAN: Hey, move over –
                I want a better view.
                I want to see that queer blood –
                Ha! Serves them right.

JODIE: Fuck right off!

WOMAN: Knew it would happen one day.
                Serves them right,
                Showing off like that
                In the street.

JODIE: Fuck you!

[She throws something offstage at the WOMAN – her lighter, maybe, if it's chunky.]

FRANKIE: I can't see anything,
                I think I've gone blind.

[A scream of panic.]

                Where's Andrew?

I want Andrew.

JODIE: Oh hush, darling. Baby.
             We'll get him when we can.

FRANKIE: I need Andrew...

[She takes out some moist tissues from her bag. She holds FRANKIE and tries to wipe his face. He winces in pain.]

FRANKIE: Don't touch me.
             I want to die.

JODIE: You know, it's lucky
             We didn't try to meet with Andrew
             After work. He would have brought the dog.

FRANKIE: You're right.

JODIE: Can you imagine? If he licked the blood
             He would go crazy –
             The dog too!

FRANKIE: Please don't try to make me laugh.

[QUEENIE reappears with a woman out of the pub. He is holding her and checking there are no patches on her clothes still burning.]

QUEENIE: I had to find a fire extinguisher,

I had to put her out,
She was on fire.
I smothered her as best I could.

WOMAN: An orange flash of fire,
A rush of warm air,
A pain like an electric shock
Right through me.

QUEENIE: Look after her –
Have you got any water?

JODIE: No.

QUEENIE: You should always carry water.
I'll find you some
If I can.

[QUEENIE exits.]

WOMAN: I looked in the pub mirror,
What was left of it –
Just a fragment.
I looked in it,
And a stranger looked back at me,
Covered in blood.
What happened?

JODIE/FRANKIE: What happened?

ALL: What happened?

[This can be a canon or round, and distributed between the four – QUEENIE should be part of it. We are stepping out of the immediate situation.]

Quartet

> How can this happen here?
> We have always felt safe here
> In Old Compton Street.
> What happened?
> We could walk down the street
> Hand in hand, and no-one turned a hair.
> We fell in and out of love,
> We quarrelled and made up.
> We could kiss in doorways,
> And policemen smiled,
> What happened?
> This was community,
> This was family,
> This was home.
> What happened?

FADE TO BLACKOUT

Scene Two

[A Hospital Bed. FRANKIE in it. His face is covered in bandages. HOSPITAL ORDERLY comes in with a cup of tea and a biscuit on a tray.]

ORDERLY: Mr Frankie? Are you awake?
            Mr Frankie?

FRANKIE: What is it?

ORDERLY: I brought you tea.
            I brought you biscuit.

FRANKIE: How the fuck do I eat a biscuit?

ORDERLY: I don't know. I no doctor,
            But everyone else have tea and biscuit.
            I don't want you feel left out.

FRANKIE: I could murder a cup of tea.

ORDERLY: I know. I get you special cup.
            They have special cups
            For cripple people
            Can't use their mouth.

FRANKIE: Thanks a bunch

ORDERLY: I get you cripple cup.

[ORDERLY exits.]

Aria

FRANKIE: Cripple cup!
              He's right of course.
              That's what I will be,
              A fucking cripple.
              Even if I get an artificial leg,
              Of course it will show,
              Everyone will know.

[He puts his hand to his face.]

              I wonder what's happening
              Underneath these bandages.
              Must be healing,
              Cos every time I smile
              I can feel the tissue pull.
              [Pause.]
              'Cripple cup!'
              There. I can feel the pull.

[QUEENIE arrives with a huge bunch of flowers.]

QUEENIE: Make way for Bossy Flossie Nightingale!
              I brought you these.

FRANKIE: What have you brought me?

QUEENIE: Flowers, darling.

             [He tries to embrace FRANKIE gently.]

FRANKIE: Careful!

QUEENIE: Sorry. I know you can't see them,
             But you can smell them
             And feel them.
             And nibble on a petal if you're peckish.
             I'm doing the rounds
             Of my poor battered babies.
             There's so many in here,
             I bought up the whole fucking florist –
             Didn't seem right to leave you out.

FRANKIE: That's what Alina said – the orderly –
             She's gone to get me a cripple cup,
             Cos that's what I'm going to be.

QUEENIE: Some of my best friends are crips –
             At least they get legless often enough.

FRANKIE: *[Trying not to laugh.]* Don't. It hurts…

QUEENIE: Then stop feeling sorry for yourself.
             You're alive. Three aren't.
             And think of poor little Alan.

FRANKIE: What's happened to him?

QUEENIE: It took his right arm off at the elbow.
             They had to amputate his left hand too.

FRANKIE: That's awful.

QUEENIE: I know. He's never going to masturbate
                again.
             I've offered to help him out
             Any time that he's short-handed.

FRANKIE: *[Laughing helplessly but painfully]*
             Don't. Don't.

QUEENIE: What else should we do?
             Can't let the fuckers get us down –
             If we do they've beaten us.

FRANKIE: Oh Queenie, you're a tonic.

QUEENIE: I'd rather be a gin.

[In FRANKIE's ear. Confidential:]

             They've got him, you know.
             Tommy Richards,
             The fucker who did it.
             Admitted it right out, and the other two,
             Like he was proud of it.
             They say that he'll get fifty years for it.

FRANKIE: When I get out,
             I'll go to church and pray for him –
             That he rots in hell.

QUEENIE: I didn't know you were religious.

FRANKIE: I'm not. Just vindictive.
             When I think of what I'd like to do to
                 him…

QUEENIE: What good does that do anybody?
             It can't change the past.

FRANKIE: That's easy for you to say.
             You won't be a freak for the rest of your
                 life
             In a wheelchair,
             Not daring to show your face.
             You won't wake up screaming
             With the nightmares.

QUEENIE: You're forgetting I was there.

FRANKIE: I'm sorry.

Aria

QUEENIE: I keep it bottled up inside
             For your sake, and the others
             In the hospital.

FRANKIE: I'm so sorry

QUEENIE: So many here.
             Some have been discharged,
             But some will take weeks.
             Months.
             Fifteen hundred nails!
             That's what they said.
             Fifteen hundred four inch nails!
             Can you imagine how much that weighs?
             Twenty kilos, maybe more.
             And that's what he brought into the bar
             With murder in his heart.
             I go into the pub, to work,
             As if nothing had happened.
             They've done it up, you know.
             You'd never realise
             That once it had been hell.
             But I see it as it was:
             The blackened walls,
             The plaster down,
             The windows out.
             Sometimes I have to have
             A vodka just to face it.
             Sometimes half a bottle.

FRANKIE: I've been so bloody selfish.

QUEENIE: You're entitled.
             Now pull yourself together,

And I will too.

[They hug, very gently. Lights fade to –]

BLACKOUT

Scene Three

[The hospital again. JODIE visiting, FRANKIE in bed, still bandaged.]

JODIE: Today's the day!
Bandages off!
I brought you some fruit
To celebrate –
They wouldn't let me bring champagne.

FRANKIE: I can't chew too well.
I lost half my teeth,
Ripped out by the nails.
I can't have false ones yet

JODIE: I know. I brought bananas.

FRANKIE: How considerate. *[Pause.]*
I wonder if I'll recognise myself?
I feel under the bandages,
I touch the scars,
And wonder what they look like.

JODIE: They'll heal.
Of course they'll heal.
Plastic surgery is wonderful
These days.

FRANKIE: Cosmetic surgery

They call it nowadays.
We've talked about it.
No way.

JODIE: You could look like Sylvester Stallone.

FRANKIE: I could look like his mother!

JODIE: Where's Andrew? He should be here.

FRANKIE: He came to see me twice,
Got too upset.
He can't deal with pain or injury,
It freaks him out.
It's the same with death –
He won't go to funerals.
His whole life is spent
Trying to hold back time.

JODIE: That's ridiculous!
He's only thirty-two...

FRANKIE: You tell him that.
He searches every day for signs of grey,
He looks for lines on his face
And fat on his body.
That's why he's always in the gym,
Always at the mirror.
I used to think he was a narcissist,
But now I know it's fear.

I told him to go home.
He was so jittery,
So anxious,
He did more harm than good.

JODIE: But even so
                You should be able to rely on him.

FRANKIE: It's not his fault.
                He wanted to be here,
                To do the proper thing,
                But then he took it out on me
                That he was feeling bad.
                No, it's best this way.

[Enter MEDIC with a wheelchair.]

MEDIC: Time for the bandages to come off, Mr.
                    Bray.
                Sorry it has been so long.

                [To JODIE:]

                We've had so many in,
                It's pushed us all to breaking point.
                I haven't seen so much destruction
                Since the IRA.

*[FRANKIE and JODIE reach for each other's hands, squeeze
tight.]*

JODIE: Can I come with him?

MEDIC: I'm afraid you can't.
            It won't take very long.

*[MEDIC helps FRANKIE off the bed and into a wheelchair.
FRANKIE is reluctant to let go. The two go to the far side of
the stage, leaving JODIE alone on the bed. During JODIE's
aria, the bandages are slowly, ritualistically taken off in full
view of the audience.]*

Aria

JODIE: It should have been me
            In that bar.
            It was all my fault.
            It was my round,
            I should have got the drinks.
            He said it was his turn
            Because I got them at the Vauxhall,
            But he bought a second round there.
            I didn't think,
            I didn't remember until later,
            And now I dare not tell him.
            He will always live with it,
            Every time he looks into a mirror
            And sees a stranger.
            Maybe he'll never walk again.
            The nails ripped the nerves to shreds
            In his legs.

Knees are so difficult to fix,
Perhaps they'll amputate.
And all because of me.
How can I look him in the face again?
Every time I will see what I have done,
And I won't be able to confess.
I don't think our friendship can survive
From so much shame.

[Lights down on JODIE. The bandages come off. We see FRANKIE's face. I don't think this should be a realistic make-up job of terrible scars. There are two ways of doing it. One is to have nothing at all, so that everything we know about the seriousness of the injuries is in other people's reaction. The other is to do a literal 'defacement', such as a big red cross across his face, as if he has been erased. This is a directorial decision.]

MEDIC: There. They're healing nicely.

[He takes some antiseptic on a pad and gently pats FRANKIE's face.]

           Just a little weepy.

FRANKIE: Can I see?

MEDIC: Is that wise?

FRANKIE: What are you saying?
           Something wrong with them?

373

MEDIC: It's a bit soon.
            Maybe you should get used to –

FRANKIE: Show me. I want to see.

MEDIC: As you wish.

[He wheels the chair to the front of the stage, to an imaginary mirror. As he goes:]

MEDIC: It's early days,
            You mustn't expect miracles.
            Ready?

FRANKIE: Yes…

MEDIC: There…

[FRANKIE looks in the mirror with horror. He breaks down wordlessly, head in hands, shoulders heaving.]

MEDIC: You must be patient.
            We can start facial reconstruction
            In a month or two.
            We must let it settle down.
            You'll be able to go home soon –
            You're lucky to be on the ground floor,
            You won't need so much adaptation.

FRANKIE: I've lost him…

I've lost Andrew,
He'll never look me in the face,
He won't be able to.
I'll make him physically sick,
Just to look at me.

MEDIC: You're still the same inside.

FRANKIE: But outside – no, it's over.
             Over.

[He looks in the mirror again.]

Take me away from this bloody mirror.

BLACKOUT

Scene Four

[FRANKIE at home in his wheelchair. There is a pair of crutches in the corner. Same 'scarring' as before. It is twelve months later. His Social Worker, JENNIFER, is looking over paperwork.]

JENNIFER: They sentenced him today.

[There is no reaction.]

Tommy Richards. The bomber.

[Still nothing.]

In court they called him Thomas,
Which made him sound almost respect-
    able.
He got four consecutive life sentences.
He said nothing.

[No reaction.]

Aren't you pleased?
Don't you care?

FRANKIE: It's too late now.

JENNIFER: I thought you would be pleased
To see justice done.

FRANKIE: Nothing can put it right.
               They could hang him
               And it wouldn't put things right.
               It won't bring Andrew back.

JENNIFER: Frankie, he's been gone now
               Almost a year.
               You must stop living in the past.

FRANKIE: Why? I haven't got a present,
               And I sure don't have a future.

JENNIFER: What happened to your nice friend –
               The one I saw here on my first visit?

FRANKIE: Jodie? Oh, she tried.
               She tried to take me out.
               'You've got to get out of yourself,'
               She said.

JENNIFER: Quite right too.

FRANKIE: Wherever you are,
               You always take yourself with you.
               We went into a pub once,
               Everybody looking at me –
               Any who could bear to look at me –
               And then the whispering:
               'Look, it's that gay bloke who was in the
                   bombing.'

Only some used other words than gay.
I couldn't stand it;
She couldn't stand it.
We ended up sitting,
Staring at each other –
We didn't know what to say. *[Pause.]*
I haven't seen Jodie in months. *[Pause.]*

JENNIFER: There are other places.

FRANKIE: Where? Where?

JENNIFER: In your community.

FRANKIE: I tried that.
One day I got desperate
For some company,
For a bit of eye candy.
Even if I couldn't have any,
I thought, no harm in looking.
I braved the rising panic that I felt,
Sitting in my chair
On the crowded bus.
The driver didn't know how to use the
    ramp –
It took ages to get off,
With everybody looking.
I went to Back Door first –
The leather club I used to go with
    Andrew –

I forgot I can't use stairs,
And they are in a basement.
So I went to Twinks, the club next door.
The doorman looked me up and down:
'We don't want your sort here.
You'll spoil people's evenings,
They come here to enjoy themselves.
The sight of you will put them off their
    drinks.
Go home. You don't belong here.'

JENNIFER: That's dreadful.
             Your own kind!

FRANKIE: My own unkind...
             What makes you think queers are so
                 wonderful?
             We're no better and no worse –
             Except the gay scene, which is worse,
             Much worse.
             Their world is full of hunks and pretty
                 boys,
             That's all they want to know –
             And the drugs of course,
             Don't forget the coke
             And the Es and the PCPs,
             The roofies and the lollipops,
             The speed and phennies,
             And the never-ending fucking.

[He comes to a hysterical climax, then calms down. JEN-NIFER strokes his hair.]

> They'd sell their grandmothers
> To get a shag.

JENNIFER: Do you want another of your pills?

FRANKIE: *[A bitter laugh.]* Another pill?
I'm no better than the rest of them.
[Pause.]
I wish Andrew had left me the dog.

JENNIFER: How could he?
How would you exercise it?

FRANKIE: Shut up! Don't remind me…

JENNIFER: Are you doing your exercises? *[She indicates the crutches.]*

FRANKIE: What's the point?

JENNIFER: You'll never get out of that chair
Unless you work at it.

FRANKIE: What do you know?

JENNIFER: You know what the physio said –

FRANKIE: She knows nothing of pain:
            [Mimics, savagely:] 'You've just got to
                ignore it
            And blast through it.'
            She can say that –
            She hasn't got nails in her legs.

JENNIFER: You have to try.

FRANKIE: Why? Where should I go?

[The doorbell rings. JENNIFER waits to see if FRANKIE will get it, almost trying to force him to move. He tries, half-heartedly. JENNIFER relents.]

JENNIFER: Shall I see who it is?

FRANKIE: [Unconvincing] There's no need.

JENNIFER: I'm nearest the door. [She goes.]

FRANKIE: Bloody do-gooders,
            Ticking their bloody boxes
            And trying to be so bloody helpful.

[JODIE comes into the room. A pause while they eye each other up, uncertain.]

JODIE: Hello –

FRANKIE: Hello –

JODIE: When I heard the news I had to come.

FRANKIE: What news?

JODIE: It was on the news –

FRANKIE: I never watch the news.

JODIE: Queenie is dead.

[JENNIFER realises that this is a private moment. To JODIE quietly:]

JENNIFER: I'll see myself out…

[JODIE nods and gestures. JENNIFER goes unobtrusively.]

FRANKIE: *[numb]* How did it happen?
             Queer bashing, of course…

JODIE: What do you mean, 'of course'?

FRANKIE: Cos that's what life is like.
             Tell me …

JODIE: It's what they call happy slapping:
             Someone cuffs you round the head,
             And someone else films it

For the internet.
It started as a joke;
The joke got out of hand.

There were five kids,
Only teenagers –
The youngest was fourteen.
Queenie was going home from clubbing
When they set on him.
It was on the South Bank,
There was no-one else around.
It was like something out of
A Clockwork Orange.

They punched him,
And threw him to the ground,
Where they kicked his head in.
It was all recorded on a mobile phone.

Someone found him an hour later;
He died in hospital –
A ruptured spleen.
They'd hit him more than forty times.

They didn't even know that he was queer.

FRANKIE: *[Exploding]* So that's all right then!

JODIE: Don't shout at me,
             It's not my fault.

FRANKIE: I loved Queenie,
             Everybody did.
             When I came home,
             He'd cleaned the place,
             Put a bunch of lilies on the table,
             Baked a chocolate cake.

JODIE: I know. I was there.

FRANKIE: He kept popping in...
             'Are you OK, chuck?
             Are you behaving yourself?
             Just checking.'
             He was like a mother.

             Where have you been?
             I've missed you.

JODIE: What could I do?
             You wouldn't let me near.
             Besides...

FRANKIE: Yes?

JODIE: I felt so guilty...
             I never told you this...
             But now with Queenie gone,
             I thought I had to.
             It should have been me,
             Sitting in that wheelchair.

I was the one who should have bought
    the drinks,
I should have been inside that pub.
It's all my fault,
Me and my memory.
It was my turn to buy the drinks.

[QUEENIE appears, a ghostly figure.]

QUEENIE: It was Tommy Richards' fault.
            Remember him?
            Stop beating up on each other,
            I won't be having it.

FRANKIE: Do you feel better now for saying that?

JODIE: Yes, yes, I do.

QUEENIE: Give her a hug.

FRANKIE: Then give me a hug. *[They embrace.]*

JODIE: Do you forgive me?

FRANKIE: What is there to forgive?

JODIE: I thought you must be thinking –
            You were brooding so,
            I thought it was preying on your mind,
            What I had done.

FRANKIE: It was – everything.
           It was all so hopeless.

QUEENIE: Now that's enough of that!

Aria

                Let me tell you something.
                A week after it happened –
                The bombing, you know –
                We'd got the rubble all cleared up,
                The windows were back in,
                But we hadn't done the painting,
                And we hadn't any stools –
                Anyway, it was just before we opened,
                There was a ringing on the bell.

                I thought it must be post,
                We'd had that many cards.
                So I answered it.

                There was these Asian lads
                Standing on the step.
                I hate to say it, but my first thought was,
                'Here comes trouble, it's happening
                    again.'
                So I went to shut the door.
                But this lad holds out his hand –
                He's got this most ginormous card –
                And he says,

'We wanted you to know,
We're all so very sorry.
We live in Brick Lane,
We use East London Mosque,
We know what it feels like.'

And one of the lads –
Handsome lad he was –
Held out his arm
To show me the scar.

Well, I cracked up,
Cried me eyes out.
These lads, well, they don't like gays
Where they come from, do they?
But here they were,
We'd all been through it…
Of course I asked them in,
And made a cup of tea.

That's what kept me going
Through the months after,
The memory of their kindness,
What we'd all been through together.

So what are you going to do now?

JODIE: So what are you going to do now?
                There'll be a funeral…

FRANKIE: I should go to that.

JODIE: There'll be hundreds there,
           You'll know a lot of them.

FRANKIE: Yes.

QUEENIE: They've all been missing you.

FRANKIE: It will bring back memories –

QUEENIE: Good ones too.

FRANKIE: They haven't seen me,
           Seen what I look like –

QUEENIE: You think they give a shit?

JODIE: Andrew may be there –

FRANKIE: I can't let him see me,
           I'll disgust him.

QUEENIE: He's changed a lot...
           Look, do you want to hope?
           Do you want a future?
           You have to believe in yourself,
           In other people,
           That they can be good.
           You have to go.

FRANKIE: You're right. I have to go.
             Give me the crutches.

JODIE: Are you sure?

FRANKIE: I'm going in there on my own two feet.

[JODIE hands him the crutches.]

QUEENIE: Don't forget to do your face.

*[JODIE finds a tissue, and takes off the 'scar' make-up.
FRANKIE is his handsome self again.]*

JODIE: You see? Skin deep.
             You're still the same inside.

FRANKIE: Let's go –

QUEENIE: Good luck, chuck.

*[QUEENIE and JODIE push the wheelchair out of the way,
so there is a bare stage. Light floods from the rear, as
FRANKIE very slowly and painfully, but determined, moves
towards it on his crutches. QUEENIE, JODIE and the
MEDIC frame him. Offstage choir – recorded – starts a Vocalise.]*

JODIE: You can do it –

QUEENIE: You can do it –

MEDIC: Have the will –

CHOIR: The world is waiting and it wants you –

JODIE: Forget the pain –

QUEENIE: This is more important.

[FRANKIE stops for a moment to get his breath back. The others are worried he's giving up.]

MEDIC: No, don't give up.

JODIE: Don't turn back.

QUEENIE: We've all got to keep going.

CHOIR: Believe, believe –

QUEENIE: Remember – you survived –

FRANKIE: I survived –

QUEENIE: You're alive –

FRANKIE: I'm alive –

JODIE: Frankie, I believe in you.

MEDIC: The doctors are so proud of you –

QUEENIE: You do my memory proud.

CHOIR: The doors are open for you.
                 Hands reach out
                 To steady and support you.
                 We have been a crime, a sin, diseased.
                 But we defy the judges and the doctor
                     and the priest,
                 We have come through A.I.D.S.,
                 Through bombs and knives and guns and
                     hate.
                 And still we come through strong,
                 And stronger yet and stronger,
                 For we are one.

JODIE/MEDIC: We're with you, with you all the way –

CHOIR: Your family is awaiting you –

QUEENIE: We are your family,
                 We always were.

JODIE: We are your family.

QUEENIE: If you come through,
                 You help to guarantee
                 I'll never be forgotten.

MEDIC: You boys inspire me so,
             Your courage is a marvel.

QUEENIE: You remember,
             You bear witness
             Even as you mourn.

[FRANKIE stops again, and feels his face with wonder]

FRANKIE: I'm alive…

CHOIR: Skin deep… skin deep…

JODIE: You are the one you always were.
             You're Frankie, and I love you.

CHOIR: We still have work to do,
             We need to work with you.
             There is work to be done,
             There are rights to be won.
             We are not there yet,
             So near yet so far.

QUEENIE: We must be kind to one another –

FRANKIE: This is the way, there is no other.

JODIE: From heart to heart
             Deep inside,
             Reach out to your people

To your tribe.

QUEENIE: Go for it, handsome,
                You're going home.

CHOIR: Home... home...
                Home is waiting for you,
                Home will welcome you;
                You're coming home.

[The music comes to a climax. Fade to –]

BLACKOUT

A Gay Century: 17

2001: Two Into One

An eighty-year love story

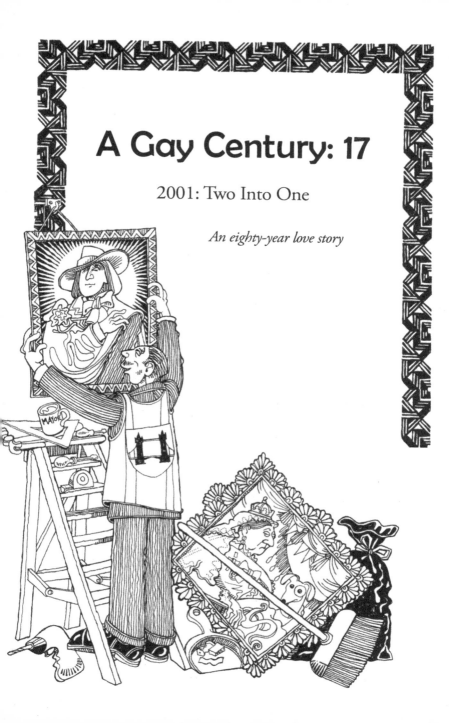

Above: *A 'gay wedding' of the 1950s*
Below: *Together for fifty years*

Introduction

One of my favourite classical/chanson singers was a Frenchman called Hugues Cuénod. Cuénod was every inch a queen, and happily welcomed in his native Switzerland as such. Switzerland introduced civil partnerships for same-sex couples in January 2007, and Cuénod seized on this to 'marry' his life partner, Alfred Augustin.

He was 105 at the time, Augustin in his 60s. Augustin said, 'Most people were happy for us, though a few promised us 15,000 years in hell.'

So the scenario here, of the civil partnership of a centenarian and the man he has been with for eighty years, is not entirely implausible, though admittedly unlikely. Civil partnerships were legislated for in the UK in 2004, and came into force a year later. However, Ken Livingstone as Mayor of London had introduced an experimental Civil Partnerships Register in 2001. The idea was to test the water, to see how much demand there was from lesbian and gay couples for formal recognition. Almost immediately there was a six-month waiting list for the service; although I leapt in almost immediately, I had to wait until late 2002 to get spliced.

The couple in this play, whose lives span almost the entire century and this opera cycle, have very similar first names – Gary and Barry – and have combined their surnames. Barry Foster and Gary Darling have become Gary and Barry Foster-Darling, but out of expediency, not principle. They are modelled on the Danes Axel Lundahl-Madsen and Eigil Eskildsen, who founded the first Danish gay rights organisation, *F-48*. This was inspired by, and named after, the 1948 United Nations Declaration of Human Rights [itself drafted by a committee chaired by a lesbian, Eleanor Roosevelt]. Axel and Eigil were the first gay people in the world to have a civil partnership when Denmark introduced them in 1989. They'd been together over forty years. To proclaim their commitment to each other, they adopted a new, combined surname, Axgil: Axel and Eigil Axgil – both a tongue-twister and a fine recipe for confusion!

It is of the essence of this piece that Gary and Barry are 'political' in a sense, but never think of themselves as political, save when goaded to it by Section 28 and the insult, enshrined in law, of saying that their 70-year relationship was 'pretended'. Otherwise, they are mainly concerned with getting on with their lives and staying out of trouble. But, as the climax of the piece says, they are two out of the anonymous thousands who by their example have created that 'Amazon of effort' which achieved liberation, more or less, over the span of a hundred years. In this opera they are visited by the ghosts of characters from other episodes in the cycle, echoing their concerns and beliefs, and also giving a sense of the flow of lives and the support of memories. In this, *Two into One* is the only vignette in Part Two where a knowledge of Part One is helpful. It's not vital, however, and I think the tenor of the drama is self-evident.

Other, more famous, people have contributed episodes

to this cycle[7], across a range of themes and musical styles, but it is the 'foot soldiers' who have done the real hard work[8], often simply by being themselves.

The story of the foot soldiers, then, is the true story of *The Gay Century.*

---

[7] *Two Queens, The Jewels, A Helping Hand, Front, Sauce for the Goose, Fishing, Home Fires, The Dog it Was that Died.*

[8] *The Berlin Boy, Separate Beds, November, After Sefton, Quarantine, A Shot at the Future, Eric Lives with Martin and Jenny, Skin Deep* – and now this.

CAST

BARRY FOSTER-DARLING: Tenor
103 years old. On a Zimmer frame. Scraggy. Obstinate, self-centred, talkative.

GARY FOSTER-DARLING: Baritone
98 years old. In a wheelchair. Fat. More emollient. Quiet. GARY and BARRY have been together since 1918.

KEN LIVINGSTONE: Baritone
Mayor of London. Late 50s. Geniality masking a certain smugness. A sharp operator.

MIRIAM MANNING: Mezzo-Soprano
40s. Livingstone's P.A., and acting Registrar. A no-nonsense woman, but with a sentimental streak beneath the carapace.

CARER: Non-speaking/singing

SETTING

The time is 2001. The foyer to the temporary Greater London Authority [G.L.A.] headquarters in Romney House, Marsham Street [City Hall is not yet ready]. An entrance through the audience. A large official portrait of Queen Victoria hangs on a wall at the back of the stage, dominating the scene. A couple of chairs and a table. An entrance offstage left to the Press Room, first aid room, etc.

INSTRUMENTS

Piano Trio: Piano, violin, cello.

TWO INTO ONE

[The action is continuous.]

[KEN is uncharacteristically nervous, waiting. MIRIAM is anxious to reassure him. She has a clipboard and a handbag.]

KEN: Where are they?
                They should be here by now.

MIRIAM: I telephoned the carer.
                They were in the taxi
                On the way from Clapham.

KEN: The traffic in this city is impossible.
                The sooner we can have a charge
                For coming into London,
                The better it will be.

MIRIAM: Here …

[She flicks some fluff off the shoulder of his jacket. KEN squirms like a small boy.]

                It will show up in the light of a flashbulb.
                We don't want readers and viewers
                Thinking you have dandruff.

KEN: Why do women always want to mother
                    me?

MIRIAM: You like it really.

KEN: Have you got my speech?

MIRIAM: Yes. Here. *[She hands it to him. He reads.]*

KEN: Historic day on the path to equality…
               Lesbians and gay men second class cit-
                   izens…
               This is but the first step to equality…
               An exciting experiment
               To test if homosexual couples
               Want public recognition of their partner-
                   ships.
               If there is a demand, it will be rolled out
               Nationally, in a civil partnership act.

               [To audience:]

               And there *will* be a demand.
               We have ceremonies booked already
               Every Saturday till Christmas.
               And there is more to come:
               After civil partnerships – gay marriage!
               [ironic] For those who want such non-
                   sense.

MIRIAM: I thought you were married.

KEN: I was, yes. That was a mistake.

I split with Christine twenty years ago.
But Kate and I will never marry now.
We've been together nearly twenty years
Without the benefit of a scrap of paper[9].
But for those who have been left out in
   the cold
So long… an affirmation.
Who are we, the majority,
To deny them what we can enjoy?
I hope 'enjoy' is meant ironically.

[He tears up the paper.]

Shit, I'll wing it. I know what I want to say.

Aria

When I was young and full of hope,
I thought that we could change the world –
And we did change the world!
We brought the people into County Hall,
The people's palace.
Gay, straight, bi, black, white, disabled –
Together we could change the world.

When I think what it was like
For all my gay friends,

---

[9] Ken Livingstone separated from Kate Allen in November 2001. He married
Emma Beal in September 2009.

When I was a lab technician
In Cancer Research.
It was still illegal,
Nearly everyone was in the closet.
People were arrested still,
Everyone in fear.

Except Bill and Stephen.
They'd been together for ten years,
A little flat near Brixton Market.
They used to let me take my girlfriends
     there,
Cos I couldn't take them home.
They did that for all their friends.
A regular knocking shop they ran!

MIRIAM: You can't say that!

KEN: Don't worry, I won't.
But I will always remember them,
And be grateful.
Bill died of A.I.D.S. in '89,
And Stephen killed himself soon after,
He couldn't live without him.

Will any of us ever know such love,
     Miriam?
I don't think I will.

MIRIAM: I couldn't kill myself for love.

KEN: Nor me.
                But I remember them.
                And when these two make promises
                And sign the register,
                Though they won't know it,
                They'll do it in the name
                Of Stephen and of Bill.

* * *

                Where are they? What is keeping them?
                Ten-thirty it was meant to be.
                The vultures are all gathered –
                They don't like being kept waiting.

                [He indicates Victoria's portrait.]

                Do we have to have that?
                It casts a total downer on proceedings.

MIRIAM: I agree. But I checked with the council.
                It's a gift from Dame Shirley Porter,
                Furniture and fittings, part of the agree-
                    ment.
                Not to be removed or changed
                Without the landlord's say-so.

KEN: Which is she?

MIRIAM: What?

KEN: Victoria. The old bat.
                Is she furniture or fitting?

MIRIAM: Look at it this way.
                The first gay wedding will spit in her eye.
                She'll be spinning in her grave.

KEN: She's too fat to spin.

MIRIAM: *[Looking at her watch again:]*
                You have the City Hall architect
                At twelve, with the revised plans.
                And the Palestinians at two.

KEN: What are their names again?

MIRIAM: Barry and Gary Foster-Darling

KEN: Sounds like they've already tied the knot.

MIRIAM: *[Consulting her notes:]*
                They changed their names by deed poll
                In nineteen thirty seven.

KEN: Sixty-three years! That can't be right.

MIRIAM: That's what it says here.

KEN: There's a role model for you!
                You and I won't clock up sixty years.

MIRIAM: It's even better than that.
            Eighty-two years!

KEN: What? That's impossible.

MIRIAM: No it's not. Don't you read your briefings?

KEN: Not if I can help it.

[He leaps from foot to foot like a little boy wanting to go the toilet.]

            Where *are* they?

            We have to get a move on.
            Already others have stolen a march.
            The Dutch have legalised gay marriage.

MIRIAM: Richard and Judy
            Married two men on the telly.
            On *This Morning* – Valentine's Day –
            Not in person, of course.

KEN: Wasn't worth a shit in law.

MIRIAM: This isn't worth a shit in law.

KEN: But worth its weight in propaganda.
            I wish I'd got in first –
            I could use the publicity.

MIRIAM: You can always use the publicity.

KEN: I'm an independent.
             I don't have Tony 'Tory Boy' Blair's
             Political machinery behind me.
             Every little helps.

[A mobile phone goes off. MIRIAM gets it out of her bag. It's an orange Nokia 3310.]

MIRIAM: Yes? *[Pause.]* At last. Show them in.

             [To KEN:] They'll be a little while, they're
                very old.

KEN: They must be. Eighty-two years!
             You see them in, and do the formal bits;
             I'll check the hacks still have some Cava
             And haven't stolen the spoons.

[Exits. MIRIAM waits nervously. Expectation building. BARRY and GARY come in from the back of the audience, and process very slowly up the aisle through it. BARRY is on a Zimmer frame, and every step is like a thunderclap as he brings it down heavily on the floor. He is followed by GARY, in a wheelchair pushed by a CARER. He has a rug over his lap, and a man bag. This mirrors the entrance of VICTORIA in 'Two Queens' at the start of the cycle. The carer is, like the page in 'Two Queens' in 1900, a silent part. GARY and BARRY argue all the way.]

BARRY: I told you we should stay away
            From Piccadilly Circus,
            But no, you wouldn't listen.
            'It's the most direct,' you said –
            As we ground to a halt in Regent Street.

GARY: It was the most direct.

BARRY: See? Stubborn as a mule.
            You know best, and none can tell you
                better.
            Just because you're in a wheelchair,
            Everyone defers to you –
            Even though you're thick as pigshit,
            You scrawny old buzzard!

MIRIAM: Do you really need to –
            Are you always like this?
            Mr Foster-Darling, the press –
            Please don't wash your dirty linen –

BARRY: Dirty linen? *[To GARY:]* Have you shat
                yourself again?

GARY: *[To MIRIAM:]* Ignore him, please.
            He's got the manners of a pig.
            Gary Foster-Darling. *[He offers his hand.]*

MIRIAM: Miriam Manning. *[She shakes it.]*
            I am acting as the Registrar.

I will do the ceremony,
Sign the certificates.
The Mayor is with the press.
He will give the City's blessing.
Of course, it isn't marriage, you realise…

BARRY: Yes it is. Marriage of inconvenience.

MIRIAM: …But it's the best that we can do.

BARRY: I don't care. I never wanted it.

MIRIAM: But surely –
I mean, you changed your names.
Gary and Barry Foster-Darling –
So romantic. *[She sighs.]*
That must count for something.
And what about your wills?

BARRY: Stop all that lovey-dovey stuff.
We're here to get tied –
Whatever you want to call it.
Nothing to do with love.

GARY: He went to Gay Liberation in nineteen
                    seventy-one,
He's never been the same.

BARRY: They were right.

[The ghosts of PENNY and WALTER, the gay activists from '1973: Autumn', appear.]

PENNY/WALTER: *We don't believe in monogamy.*

BARRY: 'A structure based on Christianity,
Whose archaic and irrational teachings
Support the family and marriage
As the pre-condition for sex.'
    – Gay Liberation Manifesto

GARY: He only went because I said
I'd had some marvellous trade
From All Saints Hall at G.L.F. meetings.
He went to Notting Hill, got his end away,
So he thought what G.L.F. said
Must be true, coming from the mouth
Of some willowy Adonis.

MIRIAM: *[To BARRY:]* So why are you doing this?

BARRY: He's in the Labour Party.
If I didn't agree
I would never hear the end of it.

[GARY fishes around in his man bag.]

GARY: Where is it? Where's my cake?

BARRY: Cake is bad for you.

Don't forget your diabetes –
All that sugar and no exercise.

GARY: I need cake when I get nervous;
                It is comfort food.

BARRY: I took it out and stamped on it.

GARY: *[Shocked]* You wasted a good Battenberg!

MIRIAM: *[To GARY:]* He's right, you know.
                You need to look after yourself.

BARRY: He never does, you know. Look at him.
                Great fat lump, neither use nor orna-
                    ment.
                I ask you, we go to all this trouble –
                And look at him!
                [To GARY:]
                There's porridge down your tie –

MIRIAM: Sugar's bad for you,
                And lack of exercise.

GARY: Don't tell me what's bad for me.
                What's bad for all us wrinklies
                Is lack of pleasure and lack of love.
                Look what lack of pleasure has done for
                    him!

BARRY: Nonsense! I am fit as a fiddle.
              Look at me. Feel that.

[He offers his bicep to MIRIAM.]

BARRY: I walk half a mile every day.
              I'm a World Record Holder, you know.

MIRIAM: [Disbelieving] What world record?

BARRY: [Proud] The over-nineties one hundred
                  metres.

GARY: You know how long that is?
              Thirty seconds!
              It's a one-hundred metre crawl,
              A one-hundred metre stagger.

BARRY: You couldn't do it. Just look at me –
              A hundred and three!

GARY: You don't look a day over a hundred.

[He attempts to turn his chair contemptuously away from
BARRY; the CARER is caught by surprise and unintentionally
hinders him.]

BARRY: Why don't you get yourself an electric
                  chair?
              Then I could pull the switch.

MIRIAM: Look, will you stop this please?
             Ken will be back any minute,
             Followed by the press and the BBC.
             You are making history today,
             And where you lead, you brave old
                 men...

GARY: I'm not brave –

BARRY: I'm not old –

MIRIAM: ...Thousands in the future will follow.
             I get quite weepy at the thought of it.

BARRY: *[To MIRIAM:]* Are you queer? Are you a
                 lesbian?

MIRIAM: *[Embarrassed]* Er – I – not really – I
                 mean,
             No – not at all – sorry about that.

BARRY: Then don't be soft, it's nothing to do with
                 you.

[KEN re-enters. To MIRIAM:]

KEN: We really must be doing this.
             I have no time to waste.
             Just a quick photo opportunity,
             Then I must go.

[*Offhand*] Is this the two old homosexuals?

BARRY: Mr Livingstone I presume? [*He thinks this is funny.*]

KEN: [*Ironic*] Very funny – how original!
You must be Mr. Foster-Darling.
May I call you Gary?

BARRY: No you may not, because I'm Barry.
[*He shouts.*]
Barry, not Gary, do you hear?
I would hate to be mistaken for
This stain-encrusted lump of lard,
This ball and chain round my existence,
This living incitement to euthanasia.

KEN: [*To MIRIAM:*] We can't have this in front of the press.

MIRIAM: Apparently they're always like this.
[*To BARRY:*] Are you going to keep this up?

GARY: It's the only thing he can keep up.

KEN: You too? This is a nightmare.
We have a responsibility to history,
We must project a positive image.

BARRY: Don't tell me what I must project.

GARY: He hasn't been able to project anything
                for years.

BARRY: I'm not a part of your P.R. machine.
                'Oh look at the old poufs,
                Aren't they sweet?
                Let's cheer up their sad old lives
                And give them a day out,
                With some meaningless certificate.
                Let's us show how marvellously
                Tolerant we are, and pat ourselves
                On the back for being so liberal.'

                I am not sweet. I am not nice.
                I rage with the frustration.

*[Enter the Ghost of VALENTINE de VERE, the old cabaret
artiste from '1973: November'. He sings:.]*

                Every day it gets more difficult
                To be Valentine de Vere.
                The stairs get steeper,
                The shops recede into the distance,
                The legs get weaker.

BARRY: I've put up with him for eighty years –
                No relief, no time off for good behaviour.
                All that comfort food,

417

The steak and kidney pudding,
The gooey spotted dick.

GARY: You could have learnt to cook yourself.

BARRY: I hate it. I hate it all.
His obsession with old musicals,
And cabaret of the twenties.
[To KEN:] He's always playing *Bitter
    Sweet,*
Or *King's Rhapsody* – nothing butch
Like *Oklahoma!* Worse, he sings along –
And he can't sing! Not a note!

[To MIRIAM:] His stupid collection of
    china –
That's another thing – you can't move
For Susie Cooper and Clarice Cliff.
And it's 'Watch where you're stepping,
Mind your feet – take your boots off –
Don't put your glasses there –'
It drives me mad.
That's it, isn't it? Old. Old. Always old.
Living in the past. You never like the new.
I remember the start of Rock 'n' Roll,
You said it didn't have a proper tune.
– But that didn't stop you going to
The Rivoli Ballroom
To chat up Teddy boys.

Well, you can stuff your All Our Yester-
days!
Sit there in your haze of nostalgia,
I am for today.

[*The Ghost of Corporal DUGGAN enters, the bandsman who loses his lover in an IRA bomb attack, from '1982: After Sefton'. He sings:*]

> *A soldier faces to the front*
> *To look life in the eyes,*
> *Both friend and foe.*
> *It will not do,*
> *Always looking back*

BARRY: I've had enough.
           I didn't come here to be insulted.

GARY: Really? Then where do you go
           To be insulted?

BARRY: This is a pointless waste of time.

[*BARRY turns on his frame and walks as briskly as he can back towards the exit.*]

GARY: You can march off a cliff for all I care.

KEN/MIRIAM: No! Come back!

GARY: It is his anger keeping him alive.
             You must remember he's in constant pain.
             All the people over eighty live with pain,
             Chronic pain, large or small.
             No wonder they get crazy mad some-
                 times.

[BARRY a little down the aisle clutches his chest, breathing very rapidly, then collapses face forward. KEN and MIRIAM rush towards him; the page goes to GARY to push him, but GARY brushes him away.]

GARY: *[Commanding:]* Leave him. He is mine,
             And only mine.

[They stand back. GARY heaves himself out of the chair and crawls on the floor to BARRY.]

             Don't die, Barry. Please don't go and slip
                 away.
             All the things I said, I didn't mean them.

[He strokes BARRY's hair.]

             We have to have a life together.
             What other life do we have?
             Darling, I'll do anything.

[There is no response.]

Do you have any alcohol in the building?

MIRIAM: You mean medical alcohol?
             I can check the medicine cabinet. *[Exits.]*

KEN: *[Rather sheepishly producing a small hip
             flask from his pocket:]*

             Will this do?
             It's a twelve-year single malt,
             Treat it with respect.

*[GARY indicates to the page to turn BARRY over. KEN helps
as necessary. GARY clumsily tips scotch into BARRY's mouth,
so it dribbles down his chin.]*

KEN: *[Protesting:]* Don't waste it!
             He's going to smell like a distillery.

GARY: Which would you rather?
             A drunk bridegroom or a dead bride-
                 groom?
             [To BARRY:] Come on, my angel, my
                 darling.

[BARRY begins to come to. Sniffs.]

BARRY: Is that – Glenfarclas?

[He reaches for the flask; GARY gives it to him. A big swig.]

It is!
60% proof!
I feel better already.

GARY: We have work to do.

BARRY: We do –

GARY: We must set a fine example –

BARRY: We must –

GARY: You must share your history –

BARRY: I must –

GARY: Our history...

BARRY: I must pass it on.

GARY: We must show our love. *[Pause.]*
You do still love me, don't you? *[Pause.]*

BARRY: I suppose so, in my own way.
After all, what else is there?

GARY: In the long run,
What else is there but love?
You may be a miserable old bugger,
But you're *my* miserable old bugger!

BARRY: I'd rather be driven to an early grave
                By you than anybody else.
                [He reaches for the whisky.] May I?

[KEN briskly removes it back into his jacket. Helps BARRY to his feet, gives him his frame.]

KEN: I think that's quite enough of that.

[MIRIAM returns with a chair.]

MIRIAM: I thought you would need this.

BARRY: I don't need that. I have my frame.

GARY: You do need it.
                Accept your limits.
                Relax.

[The CARER brings the chair to GARY. KEN and he get BARRY seated.]

KEN: Are you ready then?

GARY: I'm ready –

BARRY: I'm ready –

KEN: *[To MIRIAM:]* Let them in.

[She goes to a side door and lets the press in. They are unseen, offstage, but we see numerous digital flashes go off.]

KEN: Ladies and gentlemen of the press.
                Meet Mr Gary Foster-Darling –
                And Mr Barry Foster-Darling.

[He indicates each in turn.]

MIRIAM: These two men have been together
                Since before any of you were born.

KEN: Before your parents were born.

MIRIAM: Before your grandparents were born.

BARRY: Though I'm sure we had one or two them
                In our time.

GARY: Behave yourself!

KEN: A question from the back.
                How did you meet?

Duet

GARY: It was Armistice Day –
                Eleventh November 1918.
                He looked so dashing in his uniform.

BARRY: I was itching from the anti-lice powder.

GARY: I was only fifteen,
              And easily impressed.

*[The Ghost of the poet SIEGFRIED SASSOON, war hero
and war critic, appears, from '1918: Front'. He sings:]*

              I see my men, scrawny, famished, filthy
              White and shivering in October rain
              They strip to wash, their skin soft and silky –
              Not what you'd expect

GARY: The first we knew the war was over
              Was the noise of sirens over Lambeth.
              We thought it was an air raid,
              And rushed to shelter in the tube
              At Elephant and Castle.

BARRY: Later we defied the drizzle,
              Penetrating cold.

GARY: I was shivering in my shirt.

BARRY: I put my army greatcoat
              Round his shoulders.
              We danced in the crowds,
              Caught up in the moment.

GARY: All around us cars and buses

Piled high with people,
Making all the noise that they were able.

BARRY: It was deafening –

GARRY: We were deafening –

BARRY: All the cheering and the hooting –

GARY: The kids smashed the shop windows
              For sheer joy and delight.

BARRY: Joy and delight.
              Everybody danced the night away –

GARY: We danced the night away,
              Men with men, women with women,

BARRY: No-one gave a second thought,
              Or us a second glance.
              Later we went on to the Cavour.

GARY: So many men in powder and mascara –
              I never knew that there were others.

BARRY: We fucked in a hotel –

MIRIAM: Is that necessary?

KEN: It's what they did –

GARY: We *had carnal relations*
             At a hotel in Paddington.

*[The ghost of Corporal DUGGAN from '1982: After Sexton'
appears again. Sings:]*

GARY & DUGGAN:
             I sat there on the rumpled bed,
             And looked around the faded peeling
                 walls
             With patterns of forget-me-nots.

DUGGAN: *It was a cheap knocking shop;*
             You could take a room by the hour.
             But we had all night.
             And the next day. And night.

             I'd never let anyone do that before.

GARY: And Barry, he got Spanish flu.
             I never thought that he'd survive,
             As I watched him coughing blood.

BARRY: So many didn't.
             I lost more pals to the flu than to the
                 Boche.

GARY: But he's a stubborn bastard –

BARRY: Always have been –

427

GARY: Though he blames me still,
               Because I didn't get it
               And he did.

BARRY: No more, my love, no more.

MIRIAM: *[Taking a question:]*
               What was gay life like in the twenties?

BARRY: First to say, it was everywhere,
               If you knew where to look.
               Private clubs, public houses –

GARY: Public cottage, private party –

BARRY: There was cock to suck
               Whichever way you turned.

MIRIAM: Do you have to be so graphic?

GARY: Let us be who we are.
               We've had enough policing in our lives.

BARRY: Remember Bobby Britt and his Salome
                   dance?

GARY: Pretty Bobby Britt. So smooth…

BARRY: He lived in Fitzroy Square.
               He used to do impressions of Maud Allen –

No-one's heard of her these days –
Stripped to the waist, in harem pants.

MIRIAM: Maud Allen stripped to the waist?

BARRY: No, Bobby did.
He did Maud Allen's dance –

GARY: Salome's dance –

MIRIAM: That's in the bible.

[The Ghost of the aging LORD ALFRED DOUGLAS, Wilde's lover Bosie, appears from '1936: Front'. He sings:]

No it's not. The dance with seven veils,
That was in our play – we invented it –

GARY: He was a lovely mover,
And skin like a girl. Twenty five but
Didn't look a day more than fifteen.

BARRY: Do you remember? When his flat was
raided?
He tried to pick up the policeman
Who arrested him.

GARY: Just to embarrass the man. What balls!

BARRY: Died last year. In a nursing home.

A few days after his one-hundredth birthday.
The last one left…

GARY: There was no-one like him for sheer
               cheek.

[There is a sweet melancholy in their memory. Pause.]

               [To BARRY:] Remember the Running
                  Horse
               Near Bond Street?

BARRY: Full of gents in evening dress,
               Firemen from Marylebone,
               Bus drivers and shop boys,
               Repairmen and posties.

GARY: Mind you, it wasn't cheap –
               A shilling a pint!

KEN: How did you afford it all?

GARY: The dress suits always paid for it,
               We never had to worry.

MIRIAM: But surely you were faithful?

BARRY: We never really bothered.

GARY: Always seems more trouble than it's
               worth.

*[The Ghost of EDGAR, one of the harassed lovers from '1958:
Separate Beds', appears. He sings:]*

> *We promised that we'd always be*
> *Prepared to grant the liberty,*
> *So that the other could be free;*
> *To this we thoroughly agree.*

KEN: Question from the *Evening Standard*:
               How did you get the same names?
               Did you have some kind of marriage
               before?

GARY: Deed poll. I was Gary Foster.

BARRY: I was Barry Darling.

GARY/BARRY: I became Gary/Barry Foster-Darling.

KEN: You see, members of the Press –
               Pioneers in the fight for equality.

GARY: Pure cowardice.

KEN: *[Aghast]* What?

BARRY: Line of least resistance.

GARY: At first we said he was my Jeeves.
               I even had him registered
               As a male servant, though
               The servant tax was gone by then.

*[Enter the Ghosts of GEORGE MERRILL and EDWARD
CARPENTER, from '1912: A Helping Hand'. They sing:]*

GEORGE: *Fifteen bob a year…*

EDWARD: *Come now, George, you know*
               It's just for form's sake,
               To stop the wagging tongues.

GARY: Never really worked. He was too posh,
               And I was too common
               To have a gentleman's gentleman.

BARRY: They always rumbled.

GARY: I wasn't going to strain myself to hide it.

MIRIAM: You see? So brave…

BARRY: Bollocks. All it took was a solicitor
               And five guineas.

GARY: And tuppence stamp duty.

GARY: We were fed up being chucked out of our

432

digs,

BARRY: When the landlord or the landlady dis-
           covered –

GARY: They were always nosey –

BARRY: And always living in the ground floor flat
           Right below us.
           We got fed up with moving.

GARY: So then we thought – name change! –

MIRIAM: Husband and husband!

GARY: Not in 1937!

BOTH: Brothers!

GARY: No-one raised an eyebrow at two broth-
           ers, see,
           Who shared a flat.

BARRY: Or even a bed…

KEN: *[Ironic]* Oh, the days of innocence!

MIRIAM: What did you do in the war?
           That's the *Daily Mail* asking.

GARY: I was called up. I was thirty-seven.

BARRY: I was just too old at forty-one.

GARY: I was in the Royal Welch Fusiliers,
               Sassoon's old regiment.

MIRIAM: I thought it was illegal in the army.

*[The Ghost of MAJOR WILDER, the investigating Military
Policeman, appears from '1982: After Sefton'. He sings:]*

> *Conduct prejudicial*
> *To good order and discipline.*
> *We must make examples*
> *Of rotten apples,*
> *For other rotten apples*
> *Still lurking in the basket*

GARY: No-one gave a toss.
               I saw Arthur Marshall from Intelligence,
               Walking on a broken ankle,
               Lead his men along the Dunkirk beach
               Towards the waiting ships:
               'Come on, girls, who's on for the botany
                  walk?'
               He called Montgomery Brenda –
               Everyone called him Cynthia.

KEN: It goes to show, gay or straight,

The democracy of courage.

BARRY: Don't be so pompous.

KEN: *[Waspish]* And what did *you* do in the
                war, Barry?

BARRY: Essential war work. My lips are sealed.

MIRIAM: You can tell us now. It's all so long ago.

BARRY: Not to us it isn't.

GARY: If you must know,
                He put the pips in raspberry jam.

MIRIAM/KEN: What??

BARRY: Raspberry jam was made from swede,
                Coloured with cochineal.
                We used fine wood chips
                For the raspberry pips.
                Mixed them in to make it realistic.

GARY: So the public would swallow it –

BARRY: Literally.
                It was essential war work,
                Keeping up the nation's war morale.

[*Uncharacteristically tender*]
I was so glad when he came home…

GARY: I was so glad to get back home…

BARRY: …So I could care for him.

GARY: I was invalided out
With a leg that never set,
So I always had a limp.

BARRY: [*A joke, shared:*] A limp what?

GARY: Give over, you!

BARRY: That's why he's in the wheelchair.
But he nearly bought it twice.

GARY: You nearly bought it too,
In the flat in Finsbury Park.

BARRY: Doodlebugs, you see…

GARY: You'd hear them overhead –
Then silence –

BARRY: Where would it land?
Did it have your name on?

[*MIRIAM and KEN are transfixed.*]

GARY: It did this time.

BARRY: We were lying in bed…

GARY: I'd just come off duty
           From a twelve-hour shift.
           I was a security guard at the rifle factory
           At Enfield Lock.

BARRY: I'd cooked a shepherd's pie,
           But we fancied a bit of how's-your-father.

GARY: Later, as we lay there on the bed – Bang! –

BARRY: Direct hit on the house next door –

GARY: Brought down the front walls –

BARRY: And there we were for the whole street to
           see –

GARY: Bollock-naked on the bed –

BOTH: In the front bedroom.

[They all laugh at the image.]

MIRIAM: You could have gone to prison!

BARRY: Everybody knew us in the street,

437

Knew what we were.
We used to baby-sit
For women working in the factory,
Or on the buses.

GARY: Air Raid Warden Ennals –

BARRY: I'd had him a few times in the blackout –

GARY: You never told me!

BARRY: He found a ladder and he got us down.

GARY: We stayed with my sister and her
            husband –

BARRY: Four years till the council could rehouse
            us,
            When they put up some prefabs[10].

GARY: We lived a quiet life.

BARRY: We liked a quiet life.

GARY: We always kept ourselves to ourselves.

---

[10] Prefabricated buildings, parts built elsewhere and assembled quickly onsite.
They tackled the housing shortage created by the damage from bombs
during the Blitz. They were meant to have a life of ten to twenty years
maximum, although many lasted into the Twenty-first Century.

BOTH:	We were never anything but ordinary.
BARRY:	*[Hard]* Till the arrest.
GARY:	Suddenly the papers had all these stories, Vicars with choirboys, actors caught in toilets.
BARRY:	Remember Johnny Gielgud?
GARY:	Never liked him, too airy fairy.
BARRY:	So suddenly the people knew They weren't meant like us after all.
GARY:	The whole street changed. We didn't feel safe anymore. *[Pause.]* It was outside the Rivoli Ballroom: Three Teds were waiting On the way to Crofton Park station.
BARRY:	I was home with flu. 'Go and enjoy yourself,' I said, Hoping he'd feel sorry for me and stay.
GARY:	I didn't. Worse luck. They got me in the alley by the station, Did me over, took my wallet.
BARRY:	Two cracked ribs and a broken nose.

GARY: I crawled to Brockley cop shop.
               Only half a mile, but took me nearly half
                    an hour.

BARRY: The cops picked them up quite fast;
               They still had blood on their drapes.

GARY: They said I'd made a pass at them,
               They wanted to teach me a lesson.

BARRY: *[To MIRIAM:]* So he's the one who's
                    nicked!
               Before he's even seen a doctor!

GARY: I got nine months for importuning.
               Of course the Teds had stories all pre-
                    pared.

BARRY: They said them all the same, word for
                    word!
               A child could have seen through them.

GARY: I was landed with a lousy counsel.

BARRY: I visited him in Wandsworth nick
               Every day I was allowed.
               I always took him cake.

GARY: I always loved cake.

BARRY: I know, I know.

KEN: *[Hastily] The Guardian:* Did this turn you
                    into
                Champions for gay rights?

GARY: Not really, no.
                I didn't lose my job cos I'd retired
                Early, on account of my war wound.
                I'd got my pension;
                Could have been much worse.

BARRY: We didn't read the papers much.

GARY: We didn't have a telly till the seventies.

BARRY: When they changed the law in sixty-
                    seven
                It didn't mean so much to me.
                I was nearly seventy.

GARY: And gay rights and protesting
                    Seemed a young man's game.

BARRY: Except –

GARY: Except –

BOTH: Section 28!
                Remember that?

KEN: How could I forget?
                We're living with it still.

[The Ghost of DAME JILL KNIGHT, M.P., appears from '1988: Eric Lives with Jenny and Martin'. She sings:]

                There is shocking evidence in abundance,
                That children are being encouraged
                To be gay and lesbian,
                Some as young as five years old.
                There is a pile of filth,
                All paid for by the rates.

GARY: It was that phrase got us –

BARRY: Pretended family relationship –

GARY: How bloody dare she!

BARRY: How bloody dare she!

GARY: Seventy years we'd been together!

BARRY: How long you been married, Mrs
                   Knight?
                Forty years? Nothing!

GARY: Only march I've ever been on –

BARRY: Except you didn't march.

GARY: No, you pushed me all the way.

BARRY: I had some help, a nice young man from
               'Act-Up!'.[11]
               But I was ninety! I was knackered.

GARY: And he was drunk.

BARRY: That's true.

GARY: They hired a train from London up to
                  Manchester,
               The Campaign did; it was called the Pink
                  Express.
               They had acts busking all the carriages,
               Doing entertainment. Drag acts and the
                  like.

BARRY: And they sold pink champagne.

KEN: They knew how to protest in some style.

MIRIAM: Were you there?

KEN: I think so.

---

[11] Act-Up – AIDS Coalition to Unleash Power – was a direct action group
  working to end the pandemic and improve the lives of people living with
  H.I.V./A.I.D.S. It was founded in New York in 1987, and crossed the
  Atlantic the next year. It was the first LGBT direct action group in Britain
  since the formation of the Gay Liberation Front.

GARY: We all rolled off the train at Piccadilly,
In front of all the cameras,
In an alcoholic fog.

BARRY: What a rabble!

GARY: But we were there –

BARRY: Yes, we were there.

GARY: And we were angry –

BARRY: Yes, we were angry.

BARRY: And nobody –

GARY: Nobody –

BOTH;   Nobody –

BARRY: Was going to call my family –

GARY: My family –

BOTH: Our family –

BARRY: 'Pretend'.

[They pause, exhausted. Look at each other. Smile. Hold hands. MIRIAM hands the walking frame to BARRY. The

444

carer comes behind GARY. The three of them start walking forward.]

Finale

GARY: We are the century,
               The gay century just gone.
               We are not famous,
               Like those Queers you have known.

BARRY: You will not find us in history books,
               Or on this new, this –
               What's it called? –
               The internet

GARY: We are too small,
               We do not count as heroes,
               We are not suffragettes.

BARRY: We are not Queer Studies.
               I hate – I still hate – hate that word,
               'Queer'. It makes me shudder.

GARY: It is not our word.

BARRY: It can never be our word.

BOTH: We are too old.

[MIRIAM and KEN are at the back. KEN looks at the picture

of VICTORIA:]

KEN: I think we should —

MIRIAM: I think we should —

BOTH: And sod Dame Shirley Porter!
                        [KEN gets on the chair, which MIRIAM
                        holds. He unscrews the portrait from the
                        wall. As he does so, the voices of QUEEN
                        VICTORIA and OSCAR WILDE are
                        heard from '1900: Two Queens':-]

VICTORIA: *I will stand for something.*
                        Order. Stability. Empire.
                        Loyalty.

WILDE: *Hypocrisy*

VICTORIA: *Morality*

WILDE: *Prudery. Repression.*
                        Victorian values.
                        A stick to beat my kind
                        Down the ages.
                        And I will stand for Art.
                        The rights of Artists,
                        And for courage
                        In the face of persecution.

VICTORIA:	*Irresponsibility, dissipation* *Depravity, shallowness,* *Luxury and unreliability.*
VICTORIA:	*We have been twin pillars* *Of the century.*
WILDE:	*And my side almost won* *In the twentieth century.*
GARY:	We are two little boats, Bobbing on the Amazon of effort, The mighty tide of love.
BARRY:	Our only contribution is to be Ourselves, and nothing other.
GARY:	The mighty guns have pounded O'er our heads, and maybe we have ducked And dived from time to time.
BARRY:	But always you were never less than mine.
GARY:	But always you were never less than mine.
GARY:	And that –
BARRY:	– was adamantine

MIRIAM: We've played our part –
            A small part, true.

KEN: When pushed, and goaded
            And told what to do.

BOTH: But the fight was always yours.

GARY: We never fought.

BARRY: We were not fighters.

KEN: You were fighters, never knowing;
            Part of the army of lovers,
            Leading by example.

MIRIAM: History is not great dates of note
            Or scenes of triumph,
            Strung like pearls along the rope of time.

KEN: Every stride is made from tiny steps,
            Two forward, then one back.

MIRIAM: Daring with heart in mouth,
            Courage failing, then collected,
            To make the next, the patient step.

KEN: Suffering and sacrifice,
            Commitment and betrayal,

GARY: We are the lucky ones.

BARRY: We have survived,

GARY: We are privileged,

BOTH: We have advanced over the bones
               Of all the vulnerable and dead.
               And now we will rest.

*[An offstage chorus comes from the end of '1999: Skin Deep' –
various voices:]*

> *We still have work to do*
> *We need to work with you*
> *There is work to be done*
> *There are rights to be won*
> *We are not there yet*
> *So near yet so far*

GARY: We are old.

BARRY: We are tired.

BOTH: For us there is no work to do.

MIRIAM: Your work is only being,

KEN: And knowing of your being.

Home… home…
Home is waiting for you
Home will welcome you
You're coming home.

GARY: Yes

BARRY: Yes

CHORUS: *Home is not a private house*
                Home is a country
                Home is a state of mind

MIRIAM/KEN: Let us help you home.

GARY: I am tired now.

BARRY: It's been a long, long day.

BOTH: The shadows lengthen,
               The dark is closing in,

ALL: But as the shadows close –
               Behold the stars.

[As the music comes to a climax, MIRIAM joins GARY and BARRY's hands. KEN brings out a large portrait of OSCAR WILDE and places it on the wall where VICTORIA's had been.]

TABLEAU: THE END

A BIT ON THE SIDE

The 1980s saw the rise of the dedicated gay mega-disco, the first of which was 'Heaven' under the Arches at Charing Cross. 'The Flamingo' in Blackpool opened in 1981 [I saw Beryl Reid there, no less] and lasted more than 25 years.

THE FLAMINGO AND ALBERT:
A MONOLOGUE

There's a famous seaside place called Blackpool
That's noted for fresh air and fun.
And Mr. and Mrs. Ramsbottom,
They went there with young Albert, their son.

A grand little lad was young Albert
In his new Lycra shorts, all the rage;
And even his parents admitted
He was quite a big lad for his age.

They didn't think much of the Ocean,
The waves, they was fiddlin' and small.
There were no wrecks and nobody drownded –
Fact, nothing to laugh at at all.

They looked at the illuminations
And rode in a tram along shore.
Pa would have suggested the Zoo, but
They'd problems wi' lions before.

Young Albert was getting the fidgets –
The Attractions had left him quite cold,
And 'is stick with the 'orse's 'ead 'andle
Were a bit of a bugger to hold.

So he wandered off into the backstreets
In search of more interesting sights,
Till he came to a place called 'Flamingo',
All lit up in pink neon lights.

Inside it, the music was throbbing
Outside there was quite a chill breeze,
So Albert went up to the counter
And said, 'One half price, if you please.'

'Nay lad, there's no halves at Flamingo;
It's for adults, unwaged or wi' wage.
But seeing it's you, I'll exempt you,
Cos you are a big lad for your age.'

The dance floor was noisy and buzzin',
The place were all crowded with blokes.
It made Albert all hot and bothered,
So he left his school cap with the cloaks.

In the bar, Albert perched on a barstool
Till over the young barman came.
Albert ordered a Pina Colada,
Cos he fancied the sound of the name.

Asked Albert, 'Who are all these people?
There's so many, they can't live in town.'
'They're all queens,' said the barman, which puzzled
Young Albert, cos none wore a crown.

And when the lad took to the dance floor,
Then everyone gasped with surprise
At his stick with its 'orse's 'ead 'andle
– They'd never seen one quite that size.

Said one chap, dressed in chaps made of leather.
Yon 'orse's 'ead 'andle's a sight;
There's not many of those at Flamingo –
You should enter the Contest tonight.

Meanwhile both his parents were peckish
For fish and chips, as was their wont.
Said Pa, 'I think something is missing,
Although I can't put finger on't.'

'It's our Albert,' said Ma, 'Been abducted.
Call police,' she cried, fearing the worst.
'Nay, Ma, it's gone six,' said his father.
'We'd better have fish supper first.'

As soon as their hunger was sated
They went off in search of their son.
Pa grumbled at missing 'EastEnders',
But Ma said that it had to be done.

They enquired of a friendly policeman,
Gave description both full and complete.
'A stick with an 'orse's 'ead 'andle?
I think it went off down yon street.'

Soon they stood at the door of Flamingo,
And demanded to see the young chap.
'Yon Flamingo has eaten our Albert.'
'No, it ha'n't.' – 'Yes, it has. There's his cap.'

They pushed their way in almost brusquely
And Ma muttered darkly of Sin.
But what made the doorman most mad was
They hadn't even paid to get in.

The customers all were pressed forward
And cheering and stamping so loud
That Mother and Pa forced a passage
To see what excited the crowd.

And there, to the tune of 'The Stripper',
Young Albert was grinding onstage.
By now he'd his new Lycra shorts off –
And he was a big lad for his age.

The sight put Pa into a frenzy
And tears of rage welled in his eyes,
Though his anger were somewhat abated
After Albert had won the first prize.

A hundred-pound cheque was presented,
But before little lad could reply,
Pa said, 'I'll pocket that for safe-keeping,
And thought of th'Old Ale it would buy.'

And all of the queens from Flamingo
Went to Woolworth's the very next week
To buy sticks with an 'orse's 'ead 'andle,
The latest in discotheque chic.

And Albert is eagerly waiting
To go back, but Ma says, 'No fear.
He's not mixing with that sort of person –
We're going to My-kon-os next year.'

Acknowledgements

In the writing and rewriting of this, I benefited always from the suggestions of my composing partner Robert Ely – even if I didn't always go along with them! He has helped me tighten the dialogue and the structure immeasurably.

It has also helped to be able to hear the words in the mouths of real actors, and in the various performances of the plays which we gave on Zoom during the lockdowns of 2020–2021. For inspiring, inventive performances given in times of great stress, I wish to thank, in alphabetical order:

Peter Boyle
Mark Bunyan
Keith Bursnall
Fi Craig
Matthew Hodson
Alex Hunt
Patrick Kealey
Catherine Lord
Ian Lucas
Steve Mackay
Terry McGrath
Rex Melville
Dan de la Motte
Nicola Quinn
Lucie Spence
Rich Watkins

I'm also grateful for our Zoom audiences' comments and suggestions, and to the angels among them who contributed to the Crowdfunded kitty for paying expenses.

Chris Reilly has been a diligent proof-reader with an excellent eye for detail. The production team at Conrad Press has been, as previously, very supportive. James Essinger, the MD, has been variously encouraging, demanding, and patient in dealing with my stupid questions; as has the rest of the team. Nat and Rachael have been equally patient with my perfectionist typesetting demands; laying out plays is a fiddly and exacting challenge, to which they have risen magnificently.

The cover, and the frontispiece to each playlet, is by the incomparable David Shenton, cartoonist to the queens for nearly fifty years now, and a man I am grateful to have as a friend.

Finally, a word of thanks to my husband – for such I think him, though we don't have a marriage certificate. Without him I could not have done any of this.

Image attribution

1973: Autumn (p. 16)

Gay Liberation Front Rally 1972:
http://archives.lse.ac.uk/
Record.aspx?src=CalmView.Catalog&id=IMAGELIBRARY/1370

Quentin Crisp, 1979: Bob Workman Archive, The Bishopsgate Institute

1982: After Sefton (p. 84)

Hyde Park bombing – the seven horses killed. Daily Mail. Fair usage.
http://www.dailymail.co.uk/news/article-2211181/Facebook-message-Sefton-rider-killed-children-told-friends-hed-split-wife.html

Hyde Park Memorial to 4 bandsmen killed July 1982: Romain Behar

File:London – Regent's Park, bandstand with memorial to the bandsmen of the 1st Battalion who died on the 20th July 1982.jpg – Wikimedia Commons

1984: Quarantine (p. 142)

Newspaper headlines 1984: Author's collection

Norman Fowler and Department of Health pamphlet 1986: Press Association

1988: Eric Lives with Martin and Jenny (p. 316)

Cover of 'Jenny Lives with Eric and Martin', 1983. Public Domain

Dame Jill Knight, MP, later Baroness Knight of Collingtree. Screenshot, BBC News

1999: Skin Deep (p. 342)

The immediate aftermath of the bombing. Photo: Neil Libbert. Wikimedia Commons.

Candlelit vigil. Photo: Jonathan Garcia. Wikimedia Commons.

2001: Two into One (p. 396)

Gay Wedding 1957. Public Domain

Jimmy and Luke, Pride Parade. Photo: Flo Night. Wikimedia Commons

Some comments from readers about
A Gay Century: Volume One:

'An entertaining read. Funny and informative. We get to meet famous and eccentric characters in gay history through the lenses of well written opera librettos. Recommended.' – Amazon reader

'Peter calls these libretti 'Unreliable vignettes. They are very reliable in the pleasure and entertainment they give... His refusal to put individual gays on a pedestal, while celebrating 'landmarks' in gay history, is refreshing. All the libretti in their vastly different ways are inventive and challenging. None adopt a tone of special pleading... This whole volume is an excellent read.' – John Dixon, author of *The Carrier Bag* [Short stories] and *Seating, Finding Losing* [poems]

'Such a great book! I really loved the comical pieces, especially the one with Ernest Shackleton's brother in it [1907: The Jewels]. The portrayal of Radclyffe Hall was also a hoot. It's beautifully produced too... I look forward to the second volume.' – Mickey Silver, author of the dystopian sci-fi novel, *Olympia Heights*

'This is a collection of ten short plays. All of them are clever and interesting. They are all good. A few of them are outstanding. My favourite is 'Two Queens', set in 1900, but 'The Berlin Boy' makes a splendid companion piece to 'Cabaret'. Peter Scott-Presland has risen splendidly to the challenge of giving historical characters an ironic and incisive new script. A Gay Century is a towering achievement.' – David Gee, author of *The Bexhill Missile Crisis, Sheik-Down*, and *Lilian and the Italians*